WEDDING FLOWERS

A STEP-BY-STEP GUIDE

JUDITH BLACKLOCK

The Flower Press

Published by
The Flower Press Ltd
Marion Manor
62 Wimborne Road
Bournemouth
Dorset
BH3 7AR

Text copyright © Judith Blacklock, 2019
First published in 2019

A CIP catalogue record for this book is available from the British Library.

ISBN-13: 978 0 9935715 2 7

Design: Amanda Hawkes
Cover photograph: Thomas de Hoghton

Printed and bound in China by C & C Offset Printing Co., Ltd.

CONTENTS

INTRODUCTION

This book is for everyone who loves flowers and wants to take on a wedding for themselves, a family member or a friend. I like to think I have explained the techniques and skills that will be needed using language that is easy to understand, equipment that is easy to source and flowers that, on the whole, won't cost a fortune. Many of the designs, particularly in section one – Flowers for the Venue – can be arranged for other special occasions such as anniversaries.

LEFT A floral circlet, buttonhole and bouquet by Jo-Anne Hardy of Posy & Wild. The groom Sam Shutter has a buttonhole of *Gypsophila and Tanacetum* and his lovely bride Hannah wore a flower circlet of spray roses. The bride's bouquet includes *Freesia, Eustoma* (lisianthus) and roses from the garden, with *Eucalyptus parviflora* and *Brachyglottis*.
Designer: Posy & Wild

I have used a star system for each step-by-step design. With regard to the skills required, one star means that the design is straightforward, two that it's a little more difficult and three that you will really have to concentrate. As for the mechanics, the stars refer to how easy it is to find the equipment to recreate a similar display. I have tried to keep the components as simple as possible, but remember – with the internet, most things are readily available these days.

The images in the book have been created by me and my team at the Flower School, together with my teachers, former students and friends in the business. Many of my students have returned to their homes in different parts of the world and gone on to create bridal work second to none.

For further inspiration, look at celebrity magazines and visit your local church, register office and other places of worship when weddings are taking place. I have found that if you mingle with the guests, one side of the party will think you are with the groom and the other will think you're with the bride. Dress smartly and you may even be offered a glass of champagne!

Arranging flowers for a wedding is bound to be stressful, because they have to be perfect, but when the day is over the feeling of achievement and fulfilment is incredible and you will be all set for the next one. Be sure to take photographs so you can remind yourself just how well you have done.

Judith Blacklock

PREPARATION

Expert tips for planning the day

- Write everything down at all times. If you are planning to arrange flowers for weddings on a commercial footing get everything accepted in writing.

- Compile a list with the number of stems in each arrangement. Make sure that anyone helping also knows they have to work to this.

- Have extra foliage available to fill in gaps if the flowers come in smaller than anticipated.

- Bring more buckets than you think you will need. Florists are sometimes happy to give away black buckets free or for only a token amount. Rectangular cream buckets, often called 'Dutch' buckets, are useful and stable but more difficult to acquire.

- If you are transporting flowers, candles and foam from your home to a venue make a list and check the items off as they go into the car or van. It is so easy to forget something and then not have the time to go back and collect it. The smaller items are usually what's forgotten.

- Double-check any van hire 24 hours before the wedding.

- If you are not transporting designs in a bespoke florist's van with cords and wedges to hold them in place plan well in advance how they will travel securely.

- Take a couple of black bin bags, a brush and pan, soaked foam, knife, scissors and secateurs, a long-spouted watering can, a mister and a bottle of water with you to any venue. Having these items to hand saves a lot of time. Also take an old sheet onto which all your waste can be dropped.

- For something structural that you can't make yourself, find a professional builder, joiner or carpenter, or enlist the help of a friend or relation who is good at DIY.

- Think about parking. You cannot assume there will be spaces available, so ask first. Try and get agreement in writing. If there isn't going to be space, check out local car parks or get someone to drop you and pick you up.

- Remember that many venues are very strict about everything being collected once the wedding is over, whatever time that is. Clearing up often involves more heavy lifting and more vehicle space than you might initially think. Never underestimate the bother of doing this. At midnight on a cold wet night, without helpers, it can be a miserable task.

- If you are doing the flowers on a commercial footing be sure to charge a percentage of the overall fee for clearing after the event. This could be between 10 and 20 per cent depending on the location. Many charge more.

- If you are not yet running a business but are thinking about it, start by offering to do the flowers without payment for your time and labour, just covering your expenses. This will give you valuable experience with minimal stress. You could ask for photographs of the flowers in return for your time. Then, if you eventually decide to do wedding flowers professionally, you will have work to show in your portfolio.

- Some venues in the UK require public liability insurance. If you do not have it, check whether this will be a problem.

FLOWERS AND FOLIAGE

Expert tips for choosing the best plant material for the occasion

- Condition your flowers and foliage well before you start. This is a simple process that involves cutting about 10 percent from the bottom of the stems at an angle with a sharp knife or scissors and placing the stems immediately in clean water in a clean bucket.

- Avoid using flowers out of season, such as *Convallaria* (lily-of-the-valley) in December or *Paeonia* in November. People often want these beautiful flowers all year round, but they will usually be of poor quality and extremely expensive.

- Be aware of times when flowers cost more, such as Chinese New Year, Valentine's Day, International Women's Day, Mother's Day, Easter, Rosh Hashanah and Christmas. Even if a special flower event is taking place on the other side of the world this can affect the price of flowers thousands of miles away. There is often a strong colour association with special days or times of the year – for example, red at Christmas – so avoid these colours if possible.

- Don't use lilies for the bride and bridesmaids unless the bride insists as pollen stains are virtually impossible to remove completely. On the plus side, no flowers are such good value as open lilies in terms of size and impact in large-scale designs such as urns and pedestals. If you do get a stain don't use water to remove it; instead, try lifting it with adhesive tape and hang the garment outside on a sunny day.

- Choose flowers and foliage that are mature and robust for wired designs or situations where there is only limited or no water, such as a natural boutonnière.

- Because *Hydrangea* are large, bold and magnificent, they are superb in the sort of large-scale work that is often needed at the wedding venue.

RIGHT The herbs in this fragrant summer bouquet include *Aloysia citrodor* (lemon verbena), *Anethum graveolens* (dill) and *Eucalyptus parvifolia*.
Designer: Judith Blacklock

- For a spring wedding avoid foliage that has new growth as this will quickly go limp. When possible immerse strong green foliage under water for 30 minutes once cut. Water is absorbed through leaves as well as through stem ends, so the conditioning process is more efficient.

- Herbs are lovely in summer bouquets. My favourites are *Mentha* (mint) and *Origanum* (marjoram), which will last a surprisingly long time, lemon-scented *Pelagonium* (geranium) and *Rosmarinus* (rosemary), which is available all year round.

- Locally grown flowers are special and it is always a delight to use them for a family wedding. They look great in country-style designs but a wide selection is often limited to the main growing seasons – summer and autumn. Purchasing locally grown flowers also reduces air miles. However I do tend to mix them with a few florist's flowers – fair trade whenever possible.

In our multicultural world wedding ceremonies take place in many different venues. It might be a religious establishment such as a church, temple, synagogue or mosque. It could be a non-demoninational venue such as a hotel, register office or someone's home, or even in the open, by the river or in the woods. With this huge diversity of locations in mind, I have described floral designs that will work in a wide range of different places and can be easily adapted.

FLOWERS FOR
THE VENUE

PLANNING AHEAD

Expert tips for stylish and stress-free venue flowers

When first thinking about flowers for a wedding you need to ascertain where the guests will spend most time, as these are the best places on which to concentrate. Flowers at the entrance, either in an archway or free-standing, always look effective. During the ceremony, people will be seated and the flowers will be viewed at close quarters. After the ceremony but prior to dining, people will usually be standing for drinks so the flowers here will need to be raised in order to be seen. But don't worry, even the simplest of floral displays on the smallest budget can set the scene and enhance proceedings.

And you need not stop here. Many of the designs can be used for the anniversaries that follow.

- Before booking the venue, check when you are allowed to do the flowers. Ideally you want to bring in stands, vases and equipment and sort out the basics the day before. Some venues can be irritatingly strict and not allow this so, in an ideal world, a ceremony in the afternoon rather than the morning will give you more time on the day.

- Table centrepiece designs in water will last longer than those in floral foam. The containers used today are an important part of any design and a hand-tied bouquet in a glass vase filled with clean water will look lovely every time.

- Only place flowers on the table at the last moment if the reception is taking place in a sunny room, especially if there are a lot of glass windows that draw in the heat.

RIGHT The flowers for Table 14 included *Dianthus* 'Nobbio Violet', *D.* 'Rioja', *Gerbera* 'Black Pearl', *Gloriosa*, *Hydrangea macrophylla* 'Magical Ruby Red', *Hypericum* 'True Romance', *Jacobaea maritima*, *Paeonia* 'Red Charm', *Ranunculus* 'Azar Bordeaux', *Rosa* 'Black Baccara', *R.* 'Helga Piaget', *R.* 'Mayra's Red', *R.* 'Quicksand', *R.* 'Upper Secret', *R.* 'White Majolika', *Scabiosa* 'Blackberry Scoop', *Tulipa* 'Ronaldo', and *T.* 'World Bowl'.
Designer: Elizabeth Hemphill

- Arches of flowers look gorgeous, particularly with the bride and groom pictured beneath. If the arch faces due south and the day is sunny the flowers will need to be added the morning of the wedding, then sprayed well and regularly with water to avoid the blooms drooping. The background foliage needs to be strong and long-lasting: consider using *Buxus* (box), *Camellia*, *Gaultheria* (salal), *Prunus lusitanica* (Portuguese laurel), *Rhododendron*, *Ruscus hypoglossum* (hard ruscus) or *Taxus baccata* (yew).

- If you wish to bring in certain food items that you intend to decorate with flowers – for example, a stack of cheeses instead of the conventional cake – check with the venue first that this is possible.

- If the venue does not allow candles or night-lights, source artificial candles with flickering lights. They are excellent and can be used time and time again.

- If you are using night-lights be sure to purchase those that last 16 hours not eight. The difference in cost is minimal but it will give great peace of mind. The rate at which they burn can be slowed down by keeping them in the fridge or freezer beforehand.

- Plants and flowering bulbs last longer than cut flowers and can be taken away afterwards to be planted in the garden or displayed in the home. For a late winter or spring wedding consider putting pots of bulbs such as *Hyacinthus* in a glass cube vase, with moss tucked between the pot and the glass. These can then be placed at regular intervals down a long table.

- If the ceremony and reception are in different locations think twice before moving huge arrangements from one to the other. It is unlikely that you will have enough time to make sure they look gorgeous once they have arrived. Stems will get broken and, if you have used lilies, the carriers – who are often the ushers – may well be covered in pollen: a potentially expensive laundry issue!

- If the wedding ceremony is taking place in a religious building always discuss what you might leave. For example, if you take away the flowers from a church on a Saturday, there will probably be none for the Sunday services the next day.

- If you are arranging in a church check with the rector or vicar that the church flower arrangers are happy to allow an outside florist to do the flowers.

LEFT A stunning bridal setting at Hedsor House by Mary Jane Vaughan. Upturned circular mirrors were placed on top of large fishbowls. Posy pads were then placed on the mirror with added foam to give height. *Hydrangea* and *Delphinium* gave the floral decoration. Candles in tall, glass lanterns, interspersed with lower placements of night lights, line the aisle. These lead the eye to the magnificent display of flowers behind the table where the ceremony is to take place.
Designer: Mary Jane Vaughan

FOLLOWING PAGE ▶ Plants give strong structural design at a reasonable cost and are sustainable. After the wedding they can be planted in the garden of the bride – or whoever paid the flower bill! However, someone needs to remember to collect the plants from the venue after the wedding. Dozens of *Hydrangea arborescens* 'Annabelle' plants feature in this bold display round the water feature at Fulham Palace, by the Thames in London. They were sprayed regularly to help keep them fresh in the heat of the day.
Designer: Judith Blacklock

TOPIARY AND ARCHES

These large designs are often situated at the entrance to the venue but can also be created indoors in a large open space.

Topiary

Topiary is the art of clipping trees and shrubs into ornamental shapes. In floral design it means creating stylised shapes with the judicious placing of flowers and foliage. One of the easiest topiaries to make is a tall lollipop tree: quick and inexpensive, it will always look stunning. Two of them are often used to flank an entrance. Once you have the mechanics prepared, they can be used time and time again. Just make sure that you collect everything after the event, especially if the topiaries have been placed in attractive outer containers you don't want to lose.

The flowers and foliage you choose need to be robust and last well, particularly if the topiary is to be placed outside, exposed to the elements. My favourite flower for topiary is the spray *Chrysanthemum.* In the summer months the single white *Chrysanthemum* is as lovely as the most expensive blooms. Wild *Leucanthemum vulgare* (ox-eye daisy) can be picked from the side of the road and will work just as well as purchased *Chrysanthemum.* However, do not pick too late in the season, as insects find this flower most appetising as it matures. Stems are not the *Chrysanthemum*'s finest asset, but by placing them in a topiary sphere they will be hidden among the foliage.

EXPERT TIP

- The finished volume of flowers and foliage should be about the same as that of the container in which it is placed.

RIGHT This easy-to-make tall design was created from a pole inserted in cement with a square of floral foam at the top. White spray chrysanthemums were the star flowers interspersed through a dense covering of *Eucalyptus, Pittosporum, Skimmia* and other foliage.
Designer: Judith Blacklock

Step-by-step

Level of difficulty
Mechanics and sundries ★★
Arranging ★

Flowers and foliage
- mixed foliage such as *Arbutus unedo* (strawberry tree), *Eucalyptus*, *Gaultheria* (salal), *Hebe*, *Hedera helix* 'Arborescens' (tree ivy), *Ribes sanguineum* (flowering currant), *Viburnum tinus* or whatever you have that will stay turgid, even if in direct sun
- flowers such as spray *Chrysanthemum*, mini *Gerbera*, *Rosa* or any flowers and berries of choice. Avoid any flowers with soft or hollow stems such as *Anemone* or *Ranunculus* as they do not last in floral foam.

Mechanics and sundries
- stones or pieces of broken terracotta pot to give ballast
- plastic bucket
- quick-drying cement
- birch pole or broom handle about 1m long (3ft 3in)
- thick rubber band
- decorative outer container for your bucket with a volume similar to the ball of flowers and foliage you intend to create
- a square piece of foam or a 15–20cm (6–8in) diameter foam sphere
- about 3m (10ft) florist's polypropylene waterproof ribbon (optional)
- 0.71mm or 0.90mm wire (optional)
- ribbon scissors (optional)

METHOD

1 Place a few stones at the bottom of the bucket, leaving space at the centre so the pole can touch the bottom.

2 Follow the instructions on the packet for mixing the quick-drying cement, then pour into the bucket so that it is half full. Place the pole in the centre and hold firmly until the cement has started to set.

3 Once the mix has set, take a thick rubber band over the top of the pole and down about 5cm (2in).

4 Place the bucket in your decorative outer container.

5 Wet the foam and place it on the top of the pole, then push down firmly until it meets the rubber band and is wedged on the top.

6 Use foliage to create a sphere that is equal in volume to that of the decorative container. The first stem should be placed vertically out of the top of the foam and the second vertically downwards. The next four stems should be placed horizontally so they are equidistant from each other around the foam.

EXPERT TIP
- Plaster of Paris can be used instead of quick-drying cement. However, when water is added to plaster of Paris heat is generated, which causes expansion. This can make ceramic and terracotta crack, so use a plastic bucket for the plaster and then place it inside a more attractive container.

7 Fill in the sphere by adding more stems, all radiating from the central area (X). I like to start adding flowers when it is hard to see the foam for foliage.

8 Now add the flowers. Place the first flower at the top in the centre to create good symmetric balance. Place other flowers at regular intervals throughout. They should all radiate from the centre of the foam (X).

9 If necessary add more foliage to fill out the shape. If you are on a limited budget you could use variegated foliage (those of more than one colour, such as white and green) to give interest.

10 If you wish to add trails of waterproof polypropylene ribbon, wire the end of a doubled length of ribbon with a double-leg mount (see page 185) and insert the wire ends in the base of the foam. Tear the ribbon tails into narrow strips. Take sharp ribbon scissors and pull down against the ribbon to create curls.

RIGHT An inexpensive yet charming topiary composed of mixed foliage and peach spray *Chrysanthemum*. A swirl of waterproof florist's ribbon adds festivity and will not be damaged if the weather is inclement.

Designer: Ann-Marie French

Arches

Arches of flowers at the entrance to a venue are ideal for framing the bridal couple in photographs. Many are relatively easy to create, considering their size and impact, and all are lovely in both historic and modern venues. Choose the mechanics that are simplest for you to find and erect. As with all floral designs, they should be well thought through and stable. If you want to decorate a tall arch, scaffolding may be required. Scaffolding involves huge expense, can be dangerous to work from and there may be a limited time when it can be in place, if at all, so do check.

On a wooden frame

For this method you will need to drill into the fabric of the building so you will first need to obtain permission from the venue. If it is prohibited, then it is unlikely that a frame can be mounted and the arch will need to be free-standing.

If, like me, you are useless at DIY, ask a local carpenter or willing friend or family member to create a suitable base for the flowers. It needs to have three rings (screw eyes) in the back of the wood. One should be at the top and one at each side. Add more if necessary. These can then be hung over the embedded supports. The base also needs nails at regular intervals at the front over which the chicken wire, filled with floral foam and moss, can be hooked.

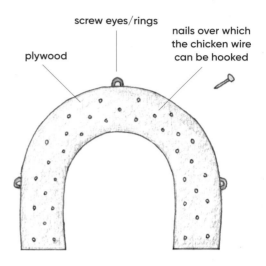

screw eyes/rings

plywood

nails over which the chicken wire can be hooked

Half arch on a wooden frame

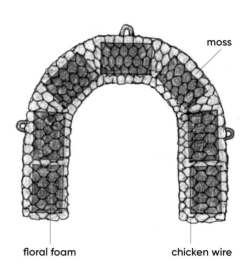

moss

floral foam

chicken wire

Half arch on a wooden frame using chicken wire, foam and moss

RIGHT AND PAGE 26 Chicken wire wrapped round floral foam and moss was suspended from a bespoke plywood frame. *Hydrangea*, *Lilium* and *Rosa* were placed through a base of *Eucalyptus* and other foliage.
Designer: Sue Adams

Step-by-step

Level of difficulty
Mechanics and sundries ★★★
Arranging ★★

Flowers and foliage
- *Sphagnum* moss
- foliage with strong stems
- flowers with strong stems in a variety of round and spray forms

Mechanics and sundries
- tracing paper
- sharp knife
- large sheet of plywood (5-ply is best)
- screw eyes/rings
- Rawlplugs
- drill
- hooks to match the screw eyes/rings
- 5cm (2in) mesh chicken wire
- floral foam
- wire or cable ties

EXPERT TIP
- *Sphagnum* is the best moss to use as it holds moisture well.

METHOD

Part A
1 Use tracing paper to make a template of the shape of the arch to be decorated.
2 Cut the plywood to shape using the template.
3 Add the screw eyes/rings to the back of the plywood.

Part B
1 Drill holes and insert Rawlplugs in the fabric of the building (if permission to do so has been obtained) where the screw eyes/rings are to go.
2 Screw the hooks into the Rawlplugs.

Part C
1 Take a piece of chicken wire the length of the arch and sufficiently wide to wrap around the foam and *Sphagnum* moss.
2 Cover the chicken wire with a thin layer of damp moss and then place the wet foam, cut to an appropriate thickness and size, on the moss. There should be gaps between the pieces to give flexibility.
3 Add more moss over the top if necessary. Wrap the chicken wire round the foam and moss to create a long flexible garland. Secure the chicken wire with wire or cable ties.
4 Insert foliage with stems sufficiently strong that can be pushed through the moss into the foam without breaking.
5 Hook the plywood arch onto the screw eyes. The nails will give additional support. Insert additional foliage so the mechanics are completely covered and add your flowers. If it is not possible to add flowers once the arch is in situ complete the design before hanging.

Using florist's spray trays with handles

Level of difficulty

Mechanics and sundries ★★

Arranging ★

This method is easy if you are allowed to have nails embedded in the arch at regular intervals. These should be sufficiently spaced so the spray trays (see page 309) do not bump into each other once hung. The trays should be filled with floral foam secured in place with pot tape.

Alternatively, use a specialist mechanic such as OASIS® Wet Foam Florette. This is a plastic tray with a handle containing foam. The foam is secured with plastic caging (see page 303). They come in various sizes and the larger ones make a secure base for a thick, opulent arch. Other brands produce a similar product.

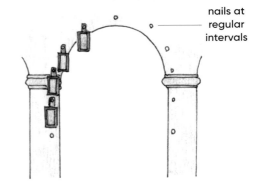

nails at regular intervals

Using florist's spray trays with handle and foam

Use the hole in the handle to hook the spray trays or Florettes over the nails and arrange your flowers and foliage. Take plant material down the sides of the plastic cages so they are hidden.

RIGHT In this arch, spray trays were attached to nails and hooks on the face of the porch. A base of foliage was created using *Euonymus*, *Photinia* and *Pittosporum* and decorated with *Alstroemeria*, spray *Chrysanthemum*, *Eryngium* (sea holly), orange and yellow mini *Gerbera* and purple *Trachelium* for a late summer wedding.
Designer: Margaret McFarlane

Using branches

If you are able to procure tall branches and two metal stands with a spike and heavy base this method is relatively quick to build. The stands need to be at least 1.5m (5ft) high.

The step-by-step for an arch using branches is described on page 31.

ABOVE AND RIGHT Branches of *Salix* (willow) were cable-tied to heavy metal stands and decorated with *Hydrangea*, a mix of roses and *Viburnum opulus* 'Roseum' in wire-netting cages containing wet foam.
Designer: Judith Blacklock

Step-by-step

Level of difficulty

Mechanics and sundries ★★/★★★

Arranging ★★

Flowers and foliage

- 2 branches of *Salix* (willow) at least 2m (6ft 6in) long
- about 60 shorter branches of willow
- foliage and flowers of choice – as this is a large-scale design the flowers need to be relatively large to have impact: bloom *Chrysanthemum*, *Helianthus* (sunflower), *Hydrangea*, open *Lilium* and orchids work well

Mechanics and sundries

- 2 metal stands with a spike and a heavy base
- heavy stones or stage weights
- cable ties
- floral foam
- 5cm (2in) mesh chicken wire
- plastic water tubes

METHOD

1 Place the metal stands in the appropriate positions. Add the stones or weights at the base to provide ballast.

2 Cable-tie a long branch to each stand. At the top of the arch angle them to follow the curve of the arch. You can join the tips together if the branches are sufficiently long.

Arch using branches

3 Add further shorter branches to the base, cable-tying them in to make secure.

4 Wrap pieces of soaked foam, of a suitable size, in chicken wire. Twist the ends of the chicken wire together to secure.

5 Cable-tie the pieces of wrapped foam to the branches.

6 Insert the water tubes into the structure. You can fill these with wet foam or water.

7 Add your foliage and flowers in the foam and the tubes.

EXPERT TIP

- Don't wrap the foam too tightly as the chicken wire will slice into it like cheese wire!

LEFT The base of this arch was a tubular structure, covered at the back with sacking and at the front with branches of *Salix* (willow) secured in place with cable ties. Foam was inserted between the branches in the lower part of the design and disguised with *Eucalyptus ovata* leaves. The base of the design was covered with 600 *Rosa* 'Deep Purple' and the upper part with 600 white and pink *Eustoma* (lisianthus). *Gypsophila* (baby's breath) was added to give a light and frothy romantic look.

Designer: Sabrina Heinen

FOLLOWING PAGE ▶ Tracy Rowbottom of Country Baskets created a magnificent rambling 4m (13ft) archway design of artificial vines, foxgloves, orchids, wild roses, thistles and mosses around the entrance of Leeds Castle. As is the case with any historic building, permanent fixings were not allowed, so Tracy positioned two sections of railway sleeper either side of the arch, with holes drilled to fit *Salix* (willow) branches. A number of these were then slotted into the holes. A frame of willow was woven across the upright branches. Liana stems were then wedged into the top of the arch and woven through. Everything was secured with cable ties.

Designer: Tracy Rowbottom

Using plants

Level of difficulty
Mechanics and sundries ★★
Arranging ★

Place each foot of a metal arch in a matching decorative container. Insert trailing plants such as *Clematis*, *Hedera helix* (ivy) or *Jasminum*, adding compost for ballast and to raise the height if necessary. Untangle trailing lengths of foliage and flowers from the plant and wrap around the arch. There are usually plenty of trails on a good-quality plant. If they are not sufficiently long, add extra stems of well-conditioned cut foliage, using cable ties to keep them in place. You can also add flowers in tubes.

Using trellis

Level of difficulty
Mechanics and sundries ★★★
Arranging ★★

A trellis frame can be cut to fit around the shape of the arch. Pieces of soaked foam can then be placed inside plastic sandwich bags and cable-tied to the trellis. Screws will need to be drilled in the fabric of the building.

Purchasing an off-the-shelf metal or wooden arch

Level of difficulty
Mechanics and sundries ★
Arranging ★★

There are many companies selling free-standing arches that are not too expensive. They often have stands/boxes on each side for ballast and quick and easy planting. The plants can then be used in the garden afterwards, making a lovely memento for the bride and groom. Less expensive arches are not self-supporting and therefore need to have the bottom 40cm (16in) in the ground or in deep pots secured with stones and compost. Check that the bride and groom will fit nicely under the arch once it is decorated.

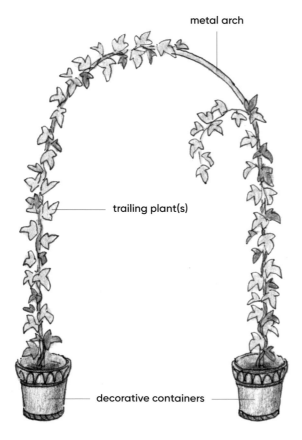

metal arch

trailing plant(s)

decorative containers

Arch using branches

Using trees

Level of difficulty

Mechanics and sundries ★★

Arranging ★★

Use tall flexible trees such as *Betula* (birch) or *Salix* (willow) at least 2m (6½ft) tall that are in tubs or planters. Tie the tips of the trees together at the top to form an arch. To add interest, wrap moss around large plastic extension tubes and bind these to the branches with cable ties. Fill the tubes with water and add your flowers.

LEFT Two *Betula* (birch) trees were planted in pots and positioned either side of the entrance to the church. The tips were bent over and secured together using cable ties. Tubes were wrapped in moss and attached to the trees at intervals, then cut roses were added to the tubes.

TOP The same design seen from inside the church.

Designer: Unknown

Using floral foam wrapped in chicken wire secured with cable ties

Level of difficulty

Mechanics and sundries ★★★

Arranging ★★

Pieces of soaked foam, wrapped in chicken wire, can be bound onto an open internal arch with cable ties. Link the gap between the foam with plant material to make a continuous arch.

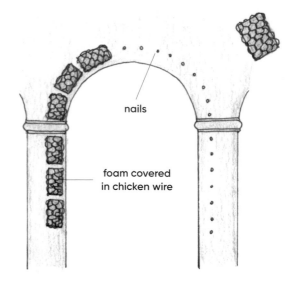

Arch using foam wrapped in chicken wire

ABOVE An arch using OASIS® Netted Foam Garlands. These were bound tightly onto the arch at regular intervals with bindwire. Juliet tells me it was not an easy task as the garlands moved round as she inserted the plant material. However, she succeeded as her garland was stunning. To decorate she used *Alchemilla mollis* (lady's mantle), *Antirrhinum, Consolida* (larkspur), *Hydrangea, Rosa* 'Avalanche' and *R.* 'Penny Lane'.

Designer: Juliet Medforth

Using floral foam garlands

Level of difficulty

Mechanics and sundries ★★

Arranging ★★

Garlands can be created using the OASIS® Netted Foam Garland or Trident Foam Ultra Garland (see page 304). Other manufacturers produce garlands suitable for small to medium arches. They need to be hung on hooks and may also require the additional support of cable ties to secure. Arrange flowers and foliage to completely obscure the floral foam and plastic or netting.

RIGHT A draped arch for an outdoor wedding. Khalida used several OASIS® Netted Foam Garlands cable-tied to the wooden frame. She created a base of *Asparagus, Danae racemosa* (soft ruscus), *Gaultheria* (salal), *Pittosporum tobira* and *Ruscus hypoglossum* (hard ruscus). She then added *Dianthus* (carnation), *Hydrangea, Hypericum* (St. John's wort), *Rosa* and spray *Rosa*.

Designer: Khalida Bharmal

HANGING DESIGNS

Hanging designs can be simple, inexpensive and easy to create whether you use a floral foam ring, a plastic spray tray, flexible twigs or a piece of pegboard as your mechanics. If you wish to suspend flowers from a ceiling it does get complicated and you will need to think carefully about how it can be done safely.

EXPERT TIPS

- If the design is placed high make sure you use long-lasting flowers or consider using artificial flowers with long-lasting fresh foliage.

- If outdoors, consider if the flowers will be in full sun. If they are they need to be placed immediately prior to the ceremony.

LEFT A simple hanging design with limited plant material in a tin vase suspended on a metal stake with a shepherd's-crook handle.
Designer: Judith Blacklock

RIGHT Hearts and flowers for a spring country wedding. The wreath was made from the twigs of *Spiraea salicifolia*. A bouquet of herbs, *Corylus* (hazel), *Lonicera* (honeysuckle) and *Tulipa* decorated the heart, but any seasonal flowers could be used as long as they are well conditioned and able to survive without water for a few hours. This bouquet was wired on at the binding point at the base of the heart. To stop it falling forward, it was also secured higher up on the central vertical strut of the wreath.
Designer: June Fray

Swags

Swags are vertical or horizontal arrangements of flowers and foliage on a suspended background which may or may not be concealed.

EXPERT TIP

- If the swag is on open work such as a grid ensure that the work is attractive from both front and back.

Using rectangles of floral foam and chicken wire

This method used foam, moss and chicken wire. It is best to soak the foam 24 hours prior to the event so there is less risk of water dripping from the foam once the stems are inserted.

Step-by-step

Level of difficulty

Mechanics and sundries ★★

Arranging ★★

Flowers and foliage

- *Sphagnum* moss
- foliage with strong stems
- flowers with strong stems in a variety of round and spray forms

Mechanics and sundries

- 5cm (2in) mesh chicken wire
- floral foam
- cable ties
- wire, twine or bindwire

METHOD

1 Lightly cover a suitable length of flat chicken wire with a thin layer of *Sphagnum* moss.

2 Place rectangles of soaked foam of a suitable size along the chicken wire and cover lightly with moss. Wrap the chicken wire firmly around the moss and foam and secure well.

3 Attach a loop of wire, twine or bindwire to the chicken wire, for hanging.

4 Decorate with flowers and foliage with strong stems, making sure that the sides are well covered.

EXPERT TIP

- If placing this swag against a wall or wallpaper first cover the back with a length of black bin liner or thin plastic film to avoid any possibility of water damage.

RIGHT All the flowers except for the *Dendrobium* orchids were arranged in foam hanging cages (see page 303) secured to the four poles of the mandap with heavy duty-clear cable ties that supported the weight of the design. The cable ties were concealed with satin ribbon that matched the drapes. After the mechanics were in place the long *Dendrobium* were inserted which established the final length of the design. The flowers used were *Dendrobium*, *Dianthus caryophyllus* 'Nobbio Violet', *D. c* 'Rioja', *Gerbera* 'Black Pearl', *Gloriosa*, *Hippeastrum* 'Liberty', *Hydrangea macrophylla* 'Magical Ruby Red', *Leucadendron* 'Safari Sunset', *Paeonia* 'Red Charm', *Phalaenopsis* 'Montreux', *Rosa* 'Black Baccara', *R.* 'Helga Piaget', *R.* 'Mayra's Red', *R.* 'Quicksand', *R.* 'Upper Secret', *Tulipa* 'Ronaldo', *T.* 'World Bowl', *Zantedeschia* 'Rudolph', with *Cordyline fruticosa* and *C.* 'Black Ti'.

Designer: Elizabeth Hemphill

Using pegboard

Pegboard is perforated hardboard and can be cut to any size to suit.

Step-by-step

Level of difficulty

Mechanics and sundries ★★
Arranging ★

Flowers and foliage

- foliage with strong stems
- flowers with strong stems in a variety of round and spray forms

Mechanics and sundries

- strip of pegboard of the required size
- wire, twine or bindwire
- glue, pot tape or cable ties
- narrow rectangles of floral foam
- thin plastic film (optional)

METHOD

1   Make a hole at the top centre of your pegboard. Take a wire, twine or bindwire through for hanging.

2   Glue, tape or cable-tie the soaked foam to the pegboard. You may wish to first wrap the faom in thin plastic film to stop it dripping.

3   Decorate with flowers and foliage of your choice.

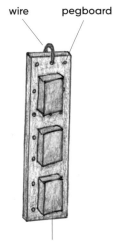

wire   pegboard

narrow rectangles of foam

LEFT A swag created on a pegboard and foam background. *Danae racemosa* (soft ruscus) and *Eucalyptus cinerea* created the outline to which *Alchemilla mollis* (lady's mantle), bloom *Chrysanthemum*, *Delphinium* and roses were added.

Designer: June Ford Crush

Using carpet grip

Carpet grip is an inexpensive but effective mechanic for a hanging design.

Step-by-step

Level of difficulty
Mechanics and sundries ★★
Arranging ★

Flowers and foliage
- foliage with strong stems
- flowers with strong stems in a variety of round and spray forms

Mechanics and sundries
- wire, twine or bindwire for hanging
- length of carpet grip
- narrow rectangles of floral foam
- pot tape or cable ties
- thin plastic film (optional)

METHOD

1 Make a hole in the top centre of the carpet grip and take a wire, twine or bindwire through for hanging.

2 Firmly strap wet foam onto the grip with pot tape or cable ties. If you wish to stop the foam dripping, first wrap it in thin plastic film.

3 Decorate with flowers and foliage of choice.

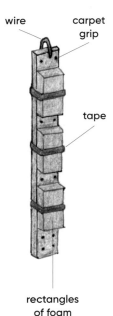

wire

carpet grip

tape

rectangles of foam

RIGHT Three cages of plastic strawberry netting covering foam were the mechanics for this swag.
Designer: Patricia Howe

Using floral foam and plastic strawberry netting

Patricia Howe devised these clever mechanics for a swag. The mechanics were three home-made cages of plastic strawberry netting, each holding a brick of foam. They were joined together with small hanging-basket 'S' hooks and secured to the wooden pillars with wire in several places.

Circular hanging designs

Rings of floral foam

Rings of floral foam are available online or from florists' sundries outlets in sizes from 20cm (8in) to 61cm (24in). They come with a backing of polystyrene or plastic. The ones with a plastic base have a lip so that water drips less readily. Those that have a polystyrene base are easier to disguise with leaves and are usually slightly less expensive.

RIGHT A hanging design of *Nigella damascena* (love-in-a-mist), David Austin *Rosa* 'Patience' and *Viburnum opulus* 'Roseum' on a base of *Heuchera* and *Physocarpus* foliage provides a warm welcome to guests.
Designer: Judith Blacklock

BELOW A foam ring covered with *Ammi* (Queen Anne's lace), spray *Chrysanthemum* and *Freesia* with *Brachyglottis*, *Euonymus*, *Hebe* and *Skimmia japonica*.
Designer: Judith Blacklock

Step-by-step

Level of difficulty
Mechanics and sundries ★
Arranging

Flowers and foliage
- foliage to cover the foam such as *Galax*, *Gaultheria* (salal), *Hedera helix* 'Arborescens' (tree ivy), *Hebe* or *Heuchera*
- round and spray flowers

Mechanics and sundries
- bindwire or other hanging material such as jute twine, metal chain or ribbon
- floral foam ring 25, 30 or 35cm (10, 12 or 14in) in diameter with either a polystyrene or a plastic base
- sharp knife

EXPERT TIPS
- Once you suspend the ring it will drip water, so place a cloth underneath.
- This design can also double up as a table centrepiece around the base of a candelabrum. Alternatively it can be filled with candles or wedding favours.

METHOD

1   Make a loop around the ring with the hanging material, allowing it to cut into the foam down to the plastic or polystyrene. Once the foam is wet it would do this anyway.

2   Wet the foam by placing the ring gently on the surface of water that is deeper than the ring. This will take about 50 seconds. Take the knife and gently remove the angular edges of the ring but don't cut too deeply.

4   Add your round flowers. These need to be placed centrally around the circle. Avoid positioning them too much to either side or their dominant form will encourage the eye to move out of the circle.

5   Fill in with other flowers, or berries, fruit or foliage if your flowers are limited. These less dominant additions should be positioned on the inside and outside of the ring.

polystyrene or plastic base

3   Cut short lengths of foliage and cover the foam, being careful to angle the leaves over the rim of the ring, both inwards and outwards. For added interest and contrast, mix your textures if you are using more than one type of foliage.

RIGHT Peonies are perhaps the most loved flowers by brides. This hanging arrangement on a floral foam ring, composed of *Paeonia lactiflora* 'Sarah Bernhardt' in full bloom combined with *Hedera helix* (ivy), is the perfect welcome for all guests and bride to the venue.
Designer: Judith Blacklock

ABOVE A circular design on a large scale complete with swing. This circular structure, sometimes called a Moongate, was encircled with OASIS® Netted Foam Garland. Eight hundred *Rosa* were placed in the foam with *Eucalyptus* and moss.

Designer: Aurélie Balyamello

RIGHT This large circle was created from 2m (6ft 6in) of aluminium wire by former student Catherine Macalpine for her son's wedding at a sheep farm in the Australian outback. Branches of *Acacia pendula* (wattle), *Atalaya hemiglauca* (whitewood or cattlebush) and *Atriplex nummularia* (saltbush) were attached to a portion of the ring, together with *Eucalyptus pleurocarpa* nuts, *Eucalyptus torquata* (coral gum) blossom and *Rosa* 'Mondial'. The ring was then hung from a tree by a sturdy rope. Ange, the bride, sat on the circle itself. It took about four hours to assemble, a lot of cable ties and many helping hands. With the benefit of hindsight, Catherine now says, 'Not a recommended activity for the morning of the wedding!'

Designer: Catherine Macalpine

Using a spray tray with handle

This arrangement, in an inexpensive plastic tray with handle (see page 309) can be hung on the back of a chair, on a wall or on a door. It can also double as a table arrangement if the handle is well hidden with flowers and foliage.

Ideally, a hanging design should be arranged in situ to ensure that it is well balanced and attractive from all sides, but it can also be made in advance.

A more expensive version of the spray tray is available which has a plastic cage over a piece of floral foam to give extra support (see page 303). Florettes are quick and easy to use and the larger versions allow for bigger designs to be created. However, they cost considerably more than the basic spray tray.

Step-by-step

Level of difficulty

Mechanics and sundries ★
Arranging ★★

Flowers and foliage

- line foliage such as *Eucalyptus*, *Gaultheria* (salal), *Ligustrum* (privet) or *Ruscus hypoglossum* (hard ruscus)
- round flowers such as mini *Gerbera* or *Rosa*
- spray flowers such as *Alchemilla mollis* (lady's mantle), *Anigozanthos* (kangaroo paw), *Hypericum* (St. John's wort) or *Solidago* (golden rod)
- filler foliage such as *Asparagus umbellatus* (ming fern), *Hebe* or *Pittosporum*

Mechanics and sundries

- sharp knife
- a quarter to a third of a brick of floral foam
- spray tray with handle
- thin plastic film (optional)
- pot tape
- hanging material such as wire, twine, bindwire or ribbon

LEFT Swags are extremely versatile. They can be suspended from walls, pew ends, a lectern or any flat surface. This hanging for a summer wedding was composed of *Bouvardia*, *Eustoma grandiflorum* 'Black Pearl' (lisianthus), *Lathyrus* (sweet pea), *Rosa* 'Sweet Dolomiti' and *Veronica*, with *Eucalyptus parviflora* and *Heuchera*.

Designer: Judith Blacklock

METHOD

1 Cut the foam to fit the tray tightly. The foam should rise about twice as high as the depth of the tray. If you are preparing this hanging design in situ water may drip on the floor when inserting your stems. To avoid this, either cover the foam with thin plastic film or wet it 24 hours in advance and allow it to dry out a little. Otherwise, just keep a cloth to hand.

2 Strap the foam firmly in place with pot tape. Avoid using too many lengths as this will reduce the usable area of foam.

3 Hang your tray in position. You can thread wire, twine, bindwire or ribbon through the hole in the handle and tie it around the sides of the pew end. Alternatively you could simply hang the tray on a nail, hook or screw.

4 Establish the depth of the design by placing the first stem (a) in the centre of the foam. The second stem (b) should be at right angles to the first and cover the spray tray's handle. The third stem (c) should extend downwards to make a design of the desired size.

5 Create a shield shape by placing short stems out of the two sides (d) to create the width of the design and further stems (e) between stems (b) and (d) and (c) and (d). They should radiate from the central area of the foam.

6 Place stems (f) out of the top of the foam so that they also radiate from the central area (X) of the foam. These stems should not be too long or the wall hanging will lose its shape. Check that there is equal distance between the stems.

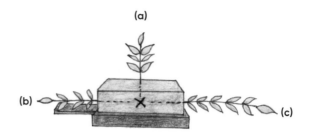

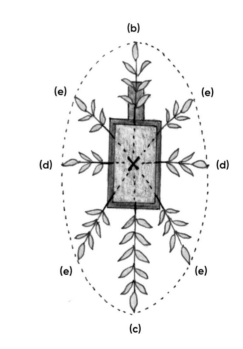

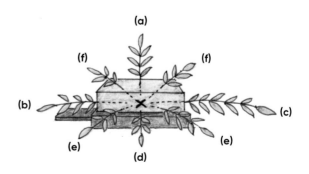

7 Create a stronger outline by incorporating more outline foliage within the foam.

8 Add your round flowers. Ensure that you have colour and flowers at the sides of the design and not just full on as the pews will be viewed from the side as people walk up and down the aisle. Consider the width of the aisle. In older churches aisles can be narrow, so make sure the flowers do not extend too far or they may damage the bride's dress.

9 Insert filler flowers through the design.

Alternative mechanics

To make suspension easier on certain pew ends, you could wrap floral foam in chicken wire and attach it to a piece of plywood with holes drilled at the top. The two holes could be threaded with wire, bindwire or similar.

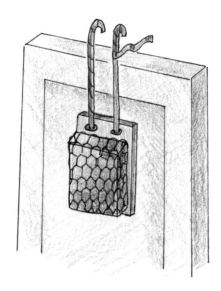

EXPERT TIPS

- You can cover the back and sides of a spray tray with long-lasting leaves such as *Hedera helix* (ivy) by fixing with cold glue.

- Ensure that any thin plastic film is secured at the bottom of the tray before anchoring with tape, as penetrating more than one layer of film can be difficult. You can make a hole with a sharp instrument such as a bradawl to allow for easier insertion of the stems.

- An effective but inexpensive mechanic for a hanging arrangement would be a supermarket food tray. Strap a piece of foam onto the tray, having made one or two holes to enable hanging. A piece of wood would also work as backing, but you would need to use a drill to make the holes.

EXPERT TIP

- If you are using wire for hanging you can wrap it in stem tape to avoid any scratches.

Garlands

Garlands are lengths of foliage and/or flowers that are flexible. They can be used to decorate ceilings, doorways, windows, ledges, arches and staircase bannisters. The making can be time-consuming but they always give great impact.

The mechanics vary in the different methods described below, ranging from a black plastic bin liner to foam, moss and chicken wire, taking in artificial *Hydrangea* on plastic matting along the way!

On a length of bin liner or rope

Bin liner is cheap, easy to disguise and readily available. If any part of the mechanics is to be seen, rope would obviously be preferred.

Level of difficulty

Mechanics and sundries ★
Arranging ★★

Flowers and foliage

- a large amount of evergreen foliage, such as *Choisya ternata* (Mexican orange blossom), *Cupressus*, *Hedera helix* (ivy) or *Pinus*, with different forms and textures

Mechanics and sundries

- large black or green plastic bin liner or length of rope
- reel wire (alternatively strong green twine can be used)
- staples (optional)
- cable ties (optional)

METHOD

1. Slit open the bin liner so that it forms a long sheet, then bundle it up to form a narrow strip. Alternatively, use a length of rope.

2. Wire a length of foliage to one end so that the tip extends beyond the end of the bin liner.

3. Add in more pieces of foliage in the same direction, angling equal amounts at each side and in the central portion.

4. If you wish to create a longer garland add further lengths of bin liner with staples or simply knot together.

5. Secure in place with wire, twine and/or cable ties.

LEFT Foliage, moss and flowers were attached to a rope which was then wrapped round the arch and secured firmly in place with cable ties. This simple decoration looked wonderful against the stone in the setting of the churchyard.
Designer: Caroline Edelin

On a length of thin plastic film and floral foam

A method that is a bit fiddly but it works well and can be achieved using household items and floral foam.

Step-by-step

Level of difficulty
Mechanics and sundries ★★
Arranging ★/★★

Flowers and foliage
- a mix of evergreen foliage

Mechanics and sundries
- thin plastic film
- tea towel
- iron
- rectangles of floral foam
- cable ties

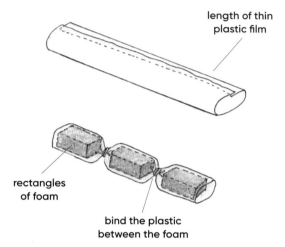

length of thin plastic film

rectangles of foam

bind the plastic between the foam

METHOD

1 Take a length of thin plastic film wide enough to hold the rectangles of foam when it is folded over. Fold the film over along the length.

2 Place a tea towel over the edges of the film and weld them together with a cool iron. Be careful with the iron's temperature: if it is too hot the plastic will burn so you may have to employ trial and error to find the right setting.

3 Slot soaked rectangles of foam into the film tube. If the garland is to be straight push the foam rectangles close together; if it is to be flexible or curved leave spaces between them. Bind the plastic film between the pieces of foam to stop them sliding together.

4 Use cable ties to secure the garland in position.

EXPERT TIP

- Keep the join of the plastic film at the back so you don't have to insert stems through two layers. If you have problems inserting stems first make a hole with a bradawl.

RIGHT Sweet, simple and very inexpensive, this garland was made on a base of thin plastic film and foam. Mixed foliage was first inserted the full length of the garland and then the single white spray *Chrysanthemum* and flowering *Viburnum tinus* was added.

Designer: Judith Blacklock

Using a ready-made floral foam garland

Use a garland of floral foam covered with green plastic netting from a specialist supplier. An excellent one is OASIS® Netted Foam Garland, available online (see page 304).

Step-by-step

Level of difficulty
Mechanics and sundries ★
Arranging ★

Flowers and foliage
- mix of long-lasting foliage
- flowers of choice

Mechanics and sundries
- netted foam garland(s)
- wire, twine, bindwire or cable ties

METHOD

1   Measure the space where you wish to have the garland to work out how many you will need. I suggest that no length should be more than about 2.6m (8ft) so that they are easier to make and transport.

2   Wet the garland. I find it best to spray with water and then spray the plant material on completion. If you soak the garland it can become too heavy.

3   Cable-tie the garland in place.

4   Cover the garland with foliage and then add flowers.

RIGHT A garland on OASIS® Netted Foam Garland cable-tied to a banister. The base of *Danae racemosa* (soft ruscus), *Eucalyptus*, *Gaultheria* (salal) and *Pittosporum* is decorated with *Chrysanthemum* 'Anastasia', *Hypericum* (St. John's wort), spray *Rosa* 'Xylene,' *R.* 'Sweet Sarah' and *R.* 'Myra'.
Designer: Khalida Bharmal

Using floral foam in plastic cages

These plastic cages are manufactured by Trident Foams and are very easy to decorate (see page 304). They contain floral foam when purchased, but once used they can be refilled with rectangles cut from one brick or more of foam.

ABOVE It is hard to believe that this garland, created by Stems & Gems, used matting of artificial *Hydrangea*. The flowers were wrapped round the banister and wired together underneath as discreetly as possible. The arrangements at the foot of the stairs were created with fresh *Hydrangea*, using about 70 blooms in each design.

Designer: Stems & Gems

ABOVE The mechanics for this garland, which continued around the entrance to the church, were plastic cages by Trident Foams.

Designer: Wendy Smith

Step-by-step

Level of difficulty
Mechanics and sundries ★★
(only because they may be difficult to find)
Arranging ★

Flowers and foliage
- a mix of long-lasting foliage and flowers

Mechanics and sundries
- cages and floral foam to cover the area required
- bindwire, twine and/or cable ties

METHOD
1 Remove the foam from the cages and soak for a few seconds. Refill the cages.
2 Secure in place with bindwire, twine or cable ties.
3 Insert short snippets of foliage so that it is hard to see the foam.
4 Add flowers of choice.

BELOW Many stems of *Danae racemose* (soft ruscus) and *Hedera helix* (ivy) were used to decorate the magnificent staircase of the Caledonian Club. The stems were out of water but lasted well for several days after the wedding. Hand-tied bunches of roses and peonies were cable-tied at regular intervals to the bannisters.

Designers: Judith Blacklock and Tomasz Koson

Using *Danae racemosa* (soft ruscus)

This is a quick, economical and effective way of using garlands to decorate a table. Here only a few flowers have been used but it is easy to create a more lavish design by incorporating more flowers. I have found *Danae racemosa* easy to grow in my garden.

The only problem with garlands around a table is making sure that they hang securely. However, event tables are often made from plywood and it is easy to insert pins to which these light garlands can be attached. See page 166 for an alternative method of decorating a table.

Step-by-step

Level of difficulty

Mechanics and sundries ★

Arranging ★

Flowers and foliage

- long stems of *Danae racemosa* (soft ruscus)
- *Cymbidium*, *Dendrobium* (Singapore orchid) and *Rosa*
- round leaves such as *Galax*, *Hedera helix* (ivy) or *Heuchera*

Mechanics and sundries

- wire, bindwire or cable ties
- pins
- orchid tubes
- double-sided tape
- decorative wire, wool, ribbon or lace (optional)

METHOD

1 Take two stems of *Danae racemosa* (soft ruscus) and entwine them, overlapping their stems and tips. They will naturally tangle up together. This can be done in the direction of preference.

2 Secure at intervals with wire, bindwire or cable ties.

3 Continue in this way to create a garland of the desired length.

4 Wire the thick ends of the *Danae racemosa* and make small loops. Hold the loops against the table where you want the garland to hang. Take pins and insert through the table cloth into the table and hang the loops. For the finer tips you can simply place the pin through the stem, through the cloth and into the plywood.

5 Wrap double-sided tape around orchid tubes. Stick leaves onto the tape. Alternatively, or additionally, you can use decorative wire, wool, ribbon or lace.

6 Insert flower heads or stems of *Cymbidium* or *Dendrobium* orchids, *Rosa* or other flowers of choice into the tubes. Use bindwire or cable ties to discreetly tie these to the garland.

***Danae racemosa* (soft ruscus)**

RIGHT A wired garland of flowers and foliage. The garland can be placed around the cake or used to decorate the wedding-cake table.

Designer: Victoria Houten

Variation
Use an OASIS® Iglu (see page 304). Wire stems of *Danae racemosa* (soft ruscus) in each end and decorate the Iglu with flowers, leaves and ribbon.

OASIS® Iglu

ABOVE
Philip attached OASIS®
Raquette Holders to the
banister and added large
OASIS® Wet Foam Florettes
from the top. The flowers
used were *Amaranthus*,
Crocosmia, *Phalaenopsis*
'Royal Peach' *and Rosa*
'Pearl Avalanche', with mixed
foliage and purple *Echeveria* plants.
Designer: Philip Hammond

Flowers from the ceiling

Images in books and magazines often have wonderful designs showing flowers hanging from the ceiling. Designs that have to be suspended need a team of people to help get them in place on beams, or equivalent, from which they can be hung. Hanging flowers from above should not be tackled by the faint-hearted!

BELOW This purpose-made chandelier dressed with *Allium, Amaranthus, Dahlia, Delphinium* and *Hydrangea* was based on a wooden ring with wet foam secured with cable ties and pot tape. It was suspended by a metal cable. The oval shape was achieved by using two semi circles and a rectangle, instead of the standard ring.

Designer: Amie Bone Flowers

Hanging basket

Hanging a basket requires long ladders and a team of strong people as the baskets are very heavy to hoist into position. You will also need horizontal supports from which to hang them and safety chains.

Step-by-step

Level of difficulty
Mechanics and sundries ★★★
Arranging ★★

Flowers and foliage
- woody foliage with strong stems
- mix of flowers with strong stems

Mechanics and sundries
- large piece of foam
- thin plastic film
- pot tape
- 3 chains of the appropriate length for hanging, with clips or similar for attaching them to the basket
- hanging basket about 55cm (22in) in diameter
- safety chain
- bradawl

METHOD

1 Soak a piece of foam large enough to fill two-thirds of the area of the basket and rise one-third of its height above the rim.

2 Wrap the foam in a single layer of thin plastic film and secure with tape. This will minimize water leaking.

3 Attach chains to the sides of the basket. You will also need a second chain for safety. This is essential. Raise the basket off the ground but not in its final position.

Note
The safety chain (not shown) should be attached to the ceiling or other support and also to the basket.

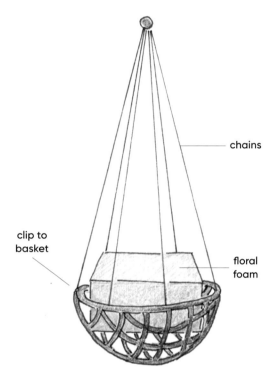

chains

clip to basket

floral foam

4 To arrange the flowers and foliage, place the first stem centrally and the second vertically down through the bottom struts of the basket. Create a sphere of plant material to the size required with a strong outline similar to that of a topiary tree (see page 22).

5 Raise the basket to its final position and double-check all is secure.

> **EXPERT TIP**
> - Use a bradawl to make holes in the film and foam for easier insertion if you are using softer stems.

RIGHT These floral hoops, twined with trails of *Hedera helix* (ivy), were suspended with nylon rope. *Eustoma* (lisianthus) and two kinds of *Rosa* provided the focal decoration on a background of *Acer* (maple) and *Eucalyptus parviflora*.

Designer: Jimmy Fu

FOLLOWING PAGE ▶
This chandelier was created on a wooden ring with wet foam secured with cable ties and pot tape. It was decorated with trailing *Amaranthus*, *Hydrangea*, *Rosa* and *Zantedeschia* (calla), with *Asparagus setaceus* (lace fern) sprayed copper, artificial and fresh foliage. Metal cables were attached at four points to the wooden ring, all of which went to a central hook. Safety chains were then attached.

Designer: Amie Bone Flowers

LARGE-SCALE DESIGNS

Large-scale designs are perfect for areas where people are standing and viewing from a distance. They can be expensive to create but if you have a garden or access to a range of foliage the cost can be greatly reduced.

ABOVE AND FOLLOWING PAGE (DETAIL) ▶ This arrangement in an urn was one of a pair near the entrance. The plant material was packed closely together and low so as not to impede the view of the flowers by the altar.

Designer: Judith Blacklock

In an ideal world make these designs where they are to be placed. Often this is not possible but they are heavy to carry so avoid attaching the bowl or urn to the base until in position.

Urns

Large arrangements are popular for both the ceremony and the reception, or where the two are combined. They are designed to be viewed from all sides, so they are ideally suited for the centre of a room. Unless you have a well-stocked garden full of plant material, you will find the cost of creating a large urn design is high.

RIGHT A large urn design to be seen in the round. The flowers used were *Delphinium*, *Eustoma grandiflorum* 'Alissa White' (lisianthus), *Gladiolus*, *Hydrangea arborescens*, *Hydrangea* 'Annabelle', *Lilium orientalis* and *Rosa* 'White O'Hara', with *Eucalyptus*, *Fagus* (beech), *Hedera helix* (ivy), *Phormium tenax* and *Xanthorrhoea australis* (steel grass).

Designer: Mo Duffill

Step-by-step

Level of difficulty

Mechanics and sundries ★★

Arranging ★★

Flowers and foliage

- linear foliage such as *Danae racemosa* (soft ruscus), *Eucalyptus*, *Fagus* (beech) or *Rhododendron*
- large, smooth-textured leaves such as *Bergenia*, *Fatsia* or *Hosta*
- tall linear flowers such as *Antirrhinum*, *Consolida* (larkspur), *Delphinium* or *Gladiolus*
- round flowers such as *Gerbera*, *Helianthus* (sunflower), *Hydrangea* or *Rosa*
- spray flowers such as *Alstroemeria*, *Eustoma* (lisianthus), *Lilium* or spray *Chrysanthemum*
- additional foliage (optional)

Mechanics and sundries

- a large piece of floral foam rather than bricks (see Jumbo foam, page 303)
- bucket to fit inside the urn
- urn – mine is 60cm (24in) tall
- plinth – mine is 70cm (27in) tall

METHOD

1 Place the foam in the bucket and insert the bucket in the opening of the urn. The rim of the bucket should be just below the rim of the urn and the foam should rise well above the rim. Place the urn on the plinth.

2 Place a stem of foliage (a) that is about the same height of the urn and foam in the centre of the foam. You could always go slightly taller if you wish.

3 Take similar lengths of foliage, but also some that are a little shorter and some that are a little longer to give variation and interest. Insert these in the foam just above the rim of the container (b), angled so they don't appear to be either dropping out of the foam or horizontal against the urn. The stem ends should be angled towards the centre of the foam (X in the diagram).

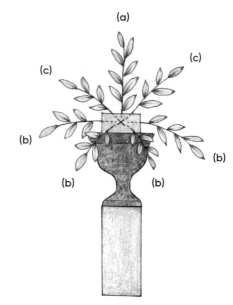

4 Take further stems (c) and insert in the top of the foam equidistant from the central stem (a) and the downwards stems (b). You need to create a strong structure before you think of adding your flowers. The stems should be approximately the same length as the central stem (a).

5 Add contrasting foliage such as *Aspidistra*, *Bergenia*, *Cordyline*, *Danae racemosa* (soft ruscus) or *Fatsia* to the structure without going beyond the shape you have already created with the first foliage. Angle all stems from the central point (X).

6 Insert the first flower centrally alongside the central stem (a). Take others through the design.

7 Choose the most dominant flowers by virtue of their colour, form or size and insert around and just below the middle of the structure you have created.

8 Add further flowers to complete your design.

EXPERT TIP

- Using a few large artificial flowers is a great way of saving money and they will last without any attention!

ABOVE A magnificent display of flowers in an urn that beautifully echoes the colours behind in the rood screen.

Designer: Neil Birks

ABOVE The arrangement of plant material in this mini urn follows exactly the same pattern as for a larger version. Here *Eucalyptus cinerea* creates the main outline with *Astilbe*, *Freesia*, small-headed *Hydrangea*, *Rosa* 'Ocean Song', *R.* 'Lovely Dolomite' and *R.* 'Dancing Clouds' completing the design. The soft muted colours of the flowers link with the stone container.
Designer: Judith Blacklock

RIGHT An urn design positioned centrally in St. Paul's Church, Knightsbridge, using *Chrysanthemum* 'Aljonka', *Hydrangea*, *Lilium* and *Viburnum opulus* 'Roseum', with *Arbutus unedo* (strawberry tree) and *Cordyline fruticosa* 'Red Edge'.

Designer: Judith Blacklock

Pedestal

A pedestal arrangement is a large-scale design suitable for any ceremony or indeed any large space. The height of a pedestal tends to range between 2 and 3m (6½ and 10ft). The symmetrical aspect of a pedestal is important as it will be viewed on three sides – from the front and from both sides. It must therefore have plenty of depth, with colour and flowers included towards and at the back. Perhaps use those at the

back that are a little less perfect in quality. If you have lots of interesting foliage you will need only a few varieties of flowers. However, if you are limited with foliage try to incorporate a wider range of flowers.

BELOW Two pedestal arrangements flanking the altar. When creating designs that balance symmetrically, it is best to divide the plant material before you start.
Designer: Mo Duffill

Step-by-step

Level of difficulty

Mechanics and sundries ★★

Arranging ★★★

Flowers and foliage

- outline foliage that is linear overall but not too narrow: good examples are *Danae racemosa* (soft ruscus), *Eucalyptus*, *Fagus* (beech), *Rhododendron* or *Sorbus aria* (whitebeam)

- large individual leaves such as *Anthurium*, *Aspidistra*, *Bergenia*, *Cordyline*, *Fatsia japonica* or *Hosta*

- additional foliage if you have limited varieties of flowers

- linear flowers such as *Antirrhinum*, *Delphinium*, *Eremurus* (foxtail lily), *Gladiolus* and long-stemmed *Matthiola* (stock)

- large round flowers such as bloom *Chrysanthemum*, *Dianthus* (carnation), *Gerbera*, *Helianthus* (sunflower), *Hydrangea*, open *Lilium* or large *Rosa*

- filler flowers and berries such as *Eustoma* (lisianthus), *Chamelaucium* (waxflower), *Hypericum* (St. John's wort), spray *Rosa* or *Solidago* (golden rod)

Mechanics and sundries

- piece from a large Jumbo block of foam (see page 303) or two standard bricks of foam

- green plastic florists' pot bowl, or a small, round washing-up bowl (approximately 25cm (10in) wide and 10cm (4in) tall is ideal for a medium-sized pedestal)

- length of 5cm (2in) gauge chicken wire to reinforce your mechanics (only needed for a very large pedestal) together with reel wire, pot tape or large rubber bands

LEFT A classic urn of flowers of *Aster*, *Brassica*, blue and white *Delphinium*, *Gerbera* and *Lilium*.

Designer: Denise Watkins

METHOD

1 Place wet foam in the plastic bowl so that it rises above the rim about one and a half times the height of the bowl.

2 If you need to use it, cut enough chicken wire to make a cap over your foam. Keep it in place with reel wire, pot tape or large rubber bands. If you are using rubber bands, loop them together under the bowl, then bring them up over the foam and wire to secure. Make sure that the chicken wire is raised above the foam and not cutting into it.

3 Add a stem of linear material (a). The length of this first stem determines the size of the completed arrangement. For an average-sized pedestal design I use a stem length of about 1m (3ft 3in). It should be placed centrally and two-thirds of the way back. This stem should lean very slightly backwards. As the majority of the stems will be placed forward, having the central stem leaning backwards creates better visual balance.

4 Place two stems (b) two-thirds the length of the first stem (a) sideways out of the central part of the exposed foam, angled slightly downwards. This flow of plant material extending below the rim of the container prevents the arrangement looking awkward on the container. A gentle curve to the plant material will make the design look more natural. You have now created the triangle ABC.

5 Add two stems (c), half the length of the first stem (a), out of the top of the foam. They should not go beyond the boundary of the triangle ABC.

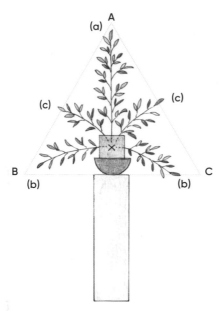

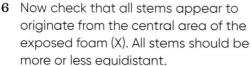

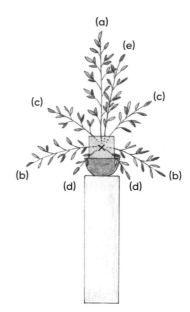

6 Now check that all stems appear to originate from the central area of the exposed foam (X). All stems should be more or less equidistant.

7 Add two short stems (d) about one-third the length of the first stem (a) at the front of the design, angled slightly downwards and outwards.

8 Give depth to the design by adding a shorter stem of foliage and/or flowers (e) behind the central stem (a), angled slightly backwards.

9 Place a short stem in the centre of the foam angled forward. This is about the same length as (d). At this point check that there is approximately the same distance between each stem.

10 Use large, smooth-textured leaves to add interest and reinforce the outline. Select some with longer stems so that they are not all at the base of the design, but are taken through the central two-thirds of the triangle. Check that the design is balanced from side to side of the central axis, from front to back and from top to bottom.

11 Reinforce the shape with line flowers, but do not go beyond the boundaries of the triangle. Take additional line flowers through the design.

12 Create the focal area with round flowers in the central two-thirds of the arrangement. I like to place the largest flower two thirds of the way from the tallest stem (a) in the centre of the design. Angle some of the flowers to give contrast and interest.

13 Complete the design with filler flowers and foliage.

EXPERT TIPS

- Ask your postman if you can have the large rubber bands that are used for keeping post together to wrap round the chicken wire if needed. These would probably be discarded otherwise.

- If you only have a white plastic bowl spray-paint it green. Always use aerosols outside or somewhere with plenty of ventilation.

Flower wall

A flower wall is gorgeous and so impressive – not to mention just perfect as a backcloth for photography of the bridal party. Creating the mechanics is time-consuming and quite labour-intensive, the cost can be high as the flowers are packed close together, but the actual arranging is easy.

BELOW AND FOLLOWING PAGE For a huge wall like this, special techniques had to be brought into play. Dennis and his partner Mick Stubbe stacked up the foam as you would a brick wall, placing thin plastic film between the bricks to prevent the water seeping out. Every three layers were covered with chicken wire stapled to the wooden base. To make absolutely sure that the bricks would not fall over or crush each other, the chicken wire was folded underneath and on top of the bricks and again stapled in place. Dennis and Mick's message is that for a construction like this you need a strong wooden base, heavy weights to keep the whole thing standing and a team of at least three people. The wall was covered with *Grevillea* and *Pistachia lentiscus* (pistach) foliage, to which *Eustoma grandiflorum* 'Alissa Apricot' and *E.g* 'Alissa Green' (lisianthus), *Dahlia*, *Hydrangea macrophylla* 'Verena Classic', David Austin *Rosa* 'Charity', *R.* 'Beatrice', *R.* 'Edith' and *R.* 'Kiera', *Scabiosa* and *Symphoricarpos* (snowberry) were added.

Designer: Dennis Kneepkens

ABOVE These images show three stages in the making of a flower wall that we made in China. It was composed of over a thousand roses inserted into designer board foam. The vertical structure, made of steel and wood, was provided by an external company.

Designer: Judith Blacklock

Step-by-step

Level of difficulty
Mechanics and sundries ★ ★ ★
Arranging ★

Flowers and foliage
- round and spray flowers to cover the wall

Mechanics and sundries
- designer board (see page 303)
- MDF backing about 2.5cm (1in) thick
- 16 screws and washers for each large designer board
- step ladder (optional)
- plastic sheeting to cover the floor
- structure to support the MDF and designer board
- stage weights or flat stones to place over the footings for extra security (optional)

METHOD

1   In Europe sheets of designer board have a polystyrene backing, making it easier to attach to MDF with screws and washers. It is very easy to cut and fit together, but try to use as many of the full-sized boards as possible. The largest you can buy are 60 x 120cm (2 x 4ft). Work out how many boards you will need for your wall.

2   To decide how many flowers you will need, get a small sample together and place your hand over them, then see how many hands' worth will fill the number of designer boards you are working with. Always have a few extra flowers.

3   Start from the bottom and attach each individual piece of designer board to the MDF backing with screws and washers. Position them as close together as possible so there are no gaps.

4   Attach the MDF to a suitable structure. You will need professional help to build this if your wall is large.

EXPERT TIPS
- Flower walls should be created in situ.
- Keep dominant white and pale colours and larger flowers more central in the design.
- Try not to push the stem ends to the very base of the foam as the water supply can be limited at this point.

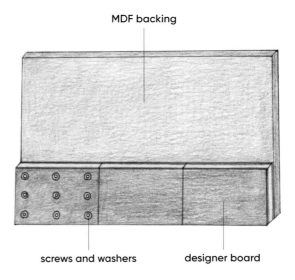

MDF backing

screws and washers   designer board

5   Start wetting the foam in the designer board. Use bottles or jugs and slowly pour the water from the top, allowing it to seep to the bottom. Protect the floor with plastic sheeting.

6   Cut the flower stems to no more than 2.5cm (1in) long, then start placing them to create a pleasing mix of colour and texture.

FOLLOWING PAGE ▶ A sustainable flower wall with a difference, created with wire mesh on a wooden frame. Small glass tubes contained *Lathyrus* (sweet pea), *Nigella* (love-in-a-mist), *Papaver* (poppy), *Vanda* orchids and *Viburnum opulus* 'Roseum'. As the wall is not solid it could also be termed a floral screen.
Designer: Natallia Sakalova

Columns

Columns can be either part of a building or free-standing. The mechanics are relatively difficult to make, so I would suggest that if you are creating your first wedding flowers you concentrate on other areas.

The columns in churches and historic buildings can look wonderful decorated if you have the time and money. Columns, which have projecting tops, are perhaps the easiest to decorate as a ring of extra-strong wire or fishing line can be wrapped around above and should not slip down. Spray trays can then be suspended from the ring of wire at regular intervals and flowers and foliage arranged in the foam to create a circle. You will need long-lasting foliage and flowers such as *Dianthus* (carnation) and *Chrysanthemum*, or artificial plant material, as watering at such a height is difficult.

Columns that are part of the building

When decorating columns that are part of the building, the following step-by-step is easy to create, providing you have a head for heights!

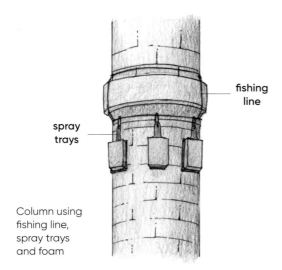

spray trays

fishing line

Column using fishing line, spray trays and foam

Step-by-step

Level of difficulty
Mechanics and sundries ★★★
Arranging ★★

Flowers and foliage
- long-lasting bushy foliage
- long-lasting flowers of choice

Mechanics and sundries
- fishing line or strong reel wire
- long ladder
- floral foam
- thin plastic film
- pot tape
- spray trays with handles

METHOD

1 Take a length of fishing line or strong reel wire around the horizontal ridge of the column, both above and then below, and check that it is secure. When using a long ladder, always make sure that there is someone holding the base.

2 Wrap pieces of foam in thin plastic film and tape into the spray trays.

3 Take further lengths of wire and thread them through the holes in the handles of the spray trays. Hang the trays at intervals from the horizontal lengths of wire so they lie flat around the pillar.

4 Angle foliage out of the foam to create a circle of plant material around the column and hide the trays. Finally add flowers to give interest.

5 Check your mechanics are secure.

RIGHT The mechanics for this swag were an oblong of plywood, slightly larger than a brick of foam, with two holes drilled at the top of the board for hanging. Dry foam was glued to the board with spray glue and taped for extra security. Because of its height, the design was decorated with artificial flowers and foliage.

Designers: Helen Drury, Jose Hutton, Julia Legg, Sue Smith, Glyn Spencer, Catherine Vickers and Betty Wain

EXPERT TIP

- Fishing line is extremely strong but you may need to pass two or three lengths through the hole in the handle of the spray tray. Check it is able to support the weight of the plant material. For everyone's safety it is essential that there is no danger of the line snapping.

Variations

- A circle of plant material like this can also be created around a square pillar.

- You could always simply cable-tie foam-filled spray trays to a column, but do get permission first.

BELOW Plastic spray trays have been suspended from a ring of wire around the column. *Anthurium*, spider *Chrysanthemum*, *Dianthus* and bridal *Gladiolus* decorated the column together with cream variegated *Euonymus*.

Designer: Emberton Flower Club

Free-standing columns

The mechanics involved in making a movable column that can be seen in the round are relatively complicated. However, once they have been constructed they can be used time and time again. This method can be successfully scaled up or down.

Step-by-step

Level of difficulty
Mechanics and sundries ★★★
Arranging ★★★

Flowers and foliage
- strong-stemmed, long-lasting foliage that can go without water for 24 hours such as *Gaultheria* (salal), *Prunus*, *Rhododendron* or *Ruscus hypoglossum* (hard ruscus)
- flowers of choice

Mechanics and sundries
- quick-drying cement
- bucket
- pole
- stones (optional)
- cable ties
- 5cm (2in) gauge chicken wire long enough to wrap round the column a few times to make sure it is secure)
- decorative outer pot
- 30cm (12in) plastic extension tubes

EXPERT TIPS
- It is advisable to create this with a friend or colleague as the chicken wire can spring back on you unexpectedly.
- Wear gloves, as chicken wire is very sharp.
- Plaster of Paris sets more quickly than cement but is usually more expensive.

METHOD

1 Mix the quick-drying cement in the bucket according to the instructions and place a pole vertically in the centre. Allow the cement to set. You may wish to place heavy stones in the bottom of the bucket to make it heavier if the column is to be placed outside.

2 Once the cement is completely dry, use cable ties to attach the chicken wire to the bottom of the pole where it meets the cement.

3 Starting at the bottom, scrunch the chicken wire around the pole and move upwards, attaching it at regular intervals with cable ties. Once at the top, go down and then back up so that you create a multi-layered base of chicken wire. Repeat for a more generous column.

4 Place the construction in a more decorative outer pot.

5 Insert extension tubes firmly between the layers of chicken wire and secure with cable ties. Half fill with water.

6 Insert the long-lasting foliage between the layers of chicken wire so the construction is covered. Insert the stems downwards and wedge them in place so that they are secure. The stem ends will not be in water. Spray the foliage well.

7 Put the flowers in the tubes.

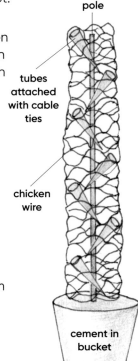

pole

tubes attached with cable ties

chicken wire

cement in bucket

Variation

This is an easier way to create a free-standing column once you have the mechanics assembled, but it will not be as impressive. You will need a wooden stake 5cm (2in) square on a flat base, or you can embed the stake in a large pot of quick-drying cement. Strap or cable-tie the extension tubes to the stake on three sides if it is to be placed against a wall or on all four sides if it is to be seen in the round. It is best to have two people doing this.

The distance between the rings of extension tubes depends on the plant material you intend to use: it needs to cover all the mechanics.

Spray the mechanics with dark green paint before adding the plant material.

wooden stake

extension tubes

flat base

ABOVE A construction of chicken wire around a wooden pole using large tubes for *Ammi* (Queen Anne's lace), bloom *Chrysanthemum* 'Anastasia', *C.* 'Sunny', *C.* 'Pjotr' and spray *Chrysanthemum* 'Green Lizard' and *C.* 'Kennedy', with *Hedera helix* (ivy), *Laurus nobilis* (bay) and *Rhododendron*.

Designer: Tomasz Koson

RIGHT This magnificent arch was created from two columns of foam wrapped copiously in chicken wire. A mass of beautiful fresh blooms decorated the columns, with artificial trailing *Wisteria* creating impact up high where watering would be difficult.

Designer: Unknown

WEDDING FAVOURS

A small gift of flowers for guests to take away does not have to cost a fortune and is a delightful reminder of a wonderful day. Here are a few innovative designs that are quick and easy to make.

Single rose

This simple design is long-lasting and can be made well in advance. It is the perfect name card or wedding favour to be taken away by the guests.

LEFT An *Aspidistra* and three *Galax* leaves cover the foam. A pink spray rose has been placed in the centre of the leaves.

Designer: Judith Blacklock

Step-by-step

Level of difficulty

Mechanics and sundries ★

Arranging ★

Flowers and foliage

- 1 *Aspidistra* leaf
- 2–3 round leaves such as *Hedera helix* (ivy), *Heuchera*, *Galax* or *Pelargonium* leaves
- 1 *Rosa*

Mechanics and sundries

- bin liner
- rectangle of floral foam 7.5 x 2.5cm (3 x 1in) – you can get 16 small rectangles from one standard brick of foam
- medium-gauge stub wire
- pearl-headed pin
- gold or silver pen to personalise the design

METHOD

1 Cut a piece of plastic from the bin liner about 5–7.5cm (2–3in) square and put it under the wet foam. Pull the plastic up around the bottom of the foam.

2 Cut the stub wire into four short lengths and bend each of these into a hairpin. Insert one in each side of the plastic to secure.

3 Feel the *Aspidistra* leaf, then remove the stalk and the part that is semi-rigid. You are going to need sufficient leaf to wrap round the foam at least one and a half times. *Aspidistra* leaves always have one side with a greater curve than the other. Hold the straighter side level with the base of the foam that is covered with plastic and wrap tightly around the foam. The shinier outside of the leaf should be facing outwards. Pin the tip of the *Aspidistra* leaf to the foam. If the leaf rises well above the top of the foam, cut it so that it is level or slightly higher than the foam. You have now created your container.

4 Take two or three round leaves. Cut the stems to about 2.5cm (1in) and insert into the foam so that they radiate out from the centre of the foam.

5 Cut the rose short, about 5cm (2in), and place centrally.

6 To personalise, write the name of the guest on one of the leaves with a gold or silver pen. If your round leaves have a rough texture write the name on the smooth *Aspidistra* that surrounds the foam.

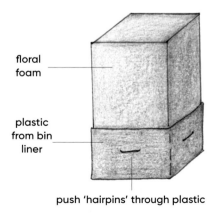

floral foam

plastic from bin liner

push 'hairpins' through plastic

bend the four sections of stub wire into hairpin shapes

EXPERT TIP

- Instead of using one large bold flower you could select a few smaller flowers and place in the top of the foam.

ABOVE A few flowers placed in opaque glasses look stylish especially when they are grouped together.

Designer: Khalida Bharmal

ABOVE *Ranunculus* massed in a silver julep cup only 10cm (4in) high. For those with a smaller budget, opaque tea-light holders would also work well.

Designer: Susan Parkinson

Succulents

Succulents are long-lasting and very fashionable. They make the perfect party favour as they keep on growing and are easy to propagate. Here are a few ideas.

- Use a *Cordyline* leaf instead of the *Aspidistra* described for the single rose design and secure with a pin and a peg. Add a succulent of your choice at the centre.

- Wrap a length of birch bark around a succulent (still in its pot) and tie with decorative wire, jute string, wool or raffia. Look for succulents with interesting shapes.

- Have a tray of mini succulents at the exit for guests to take as they leave.

EXPERT TIP

- Succulents are easy to propagate. Simply remove the individual leaves at the bottom of the plant complete with base. Allow the ends to dry out a little and place them horizontally on top of well-draining succulent or cactus soil. Roots will appear first and then baby plants. Pot-on in gritty compost.

ABOVE Easy inexpensive party favours that last. Succulents can be given as party favours in a wide range of containers and with a wrap of leaves, bark, ribbon, wool or fabric. If using a wooden peg to keep the wrap in place, why not write the wedding guests' name on it? Alternatively, the name can be written on a brown paper luggage label threaded on string or raffia.
Designer: Marco Wamelink

Cellophane parcels

These quick and easy party favours are complete in themselves, so there's no container to think about. If you create one for each guest there will also be no need for a central placement of flowers. Use flowers and foliage of your choice.

Step-by-step

Level of difficulty
Mechanics and sundries ★
Arranging ★

Mechanics and sundries
- square of patterned or opaque cellophane
- a third of a brick of floral foam
- rubber band
- raffia or ribbon

METHOD

1   Take a square of cellophane and fold into smaller and smaller triangles until you have a shape rather like an ice-cream cone. Cut about 60 per cent from the top. When you open up the cellophane you will have a wavy circle.

2   Place the piece of wet foam in the centre of the cellophane and bring up the sides. Take the rubber band about two-thirds up the sides of the foam and cover with raffia or ribbon. Once secure you can cut away the rubber band.

3   Add flowers and foliage to cover your foam.

4   If you wish, you could include a heart shape on a stick bearing the names of the couple.

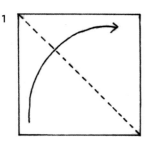

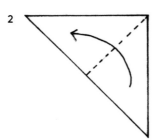

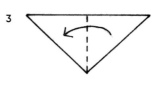

ABOVE This party favour, of flowers in foam with a cellophane wrap, is inexpensive to make and light to carry home, with no worry that the water might spill.
Designer: Judith Blacklock

Cones of dried flowers and herbs

Cones of dried flowers make delightful gifts to take away and will give fragrance to the home for months to come. They can also be used as confetti. Dry flowers and herbs when the weather is hot and the process will be quick and effective. Experiment and use any flower you have to hand, but I recommend those that have relatively small petals and have strong clear colours.

Step-by-step

Level of difficulty

Mechanics and sundries ★

Arranging ★

Flowers and foliage

- *Calendula, Cosmos, Dahlia, Delphinium, Hydrangea, Lavendula, Paeonia*, small to medium *Rosa, Pelargonium* and *Viola* with *Mentha* (mint) and *Rosmarinus* (rosemary)
- natural fragrance essence

Mechanics and sundries

- thick sheets of A4 paper
- double-sided tape
- ribbon (optional)

METHOD

1 Remove the petals from the *Rosa*, the individual florets from the *Delphinium* and the leaves and flowers from the herbs. Garden roses are ideal, as the petals are usually smaller and often have fragrance.

2 Place on tin trays and leave on a south-facing window ledge. If the weather is warm and sunny the plant material should dry in a few days. Alternatively, place close to a radiator in the later months of the year. Keep turning regularly. The tin trays radiate heat from below.

3 As each tray of plant material dries, place the contents in an air-tight box.

4 Add natural fragrance essence to extend the life of the wonderful natural smells.

5 To make a paper cone take a sheet of A4 paper and cut it into a diamond shape. Roll it along the widest side to form a cone and secure with double-sided tape. Attach ribbon with glue if so wished.

EXPERT TIPS

- Use only petals that are perfect.
- Keep the lid tightly shut on the fragrance bottle as it will evaporate quickly.
- You can buy cones for confetti online, or why not copy a sheet of music or an illustrated manuscript?

ABOVE AND LEFT Making confetti is easy and rewarding. Try all the petals you can find – the research is fascinating.
Designer: Judith Blacklock

Gift boxes

Giving gift boxes at weddings is extremely popular in many parts of the world and is a lovely way to thank people for coming. They are incredibly easy to make but rely for their effect on the careful choice of flower shapes and textures. You can use any plain box or cover one that is branded with pressed *Eucalyptus*, *Ruscus hypoglossum* (hard ruscus) or *Stachys byzantina* (lamb's ear) leaves. Blank gift boxes can be ordered on line.

RIGHT Gift boxes are so easy to create. Just make sure there is a waterproof lining and avoid filling with more wet foam than you need, as this will make the box heavy to carry. Good textural contrasts are important because there is little or no space between the elements.

Designer: Judith Blacklock

Step-by-step

Level of difficulty

Mechanics and sundries ★

Arranging ★

Flowers and foliage

- a mix of flowers with different forms and textures
- neat foliage to fill in the gaps such as *Asparagus umbellatus* (ming fern) or small-leaved *Hebe*

Mechanics and sundries

- round or square box, not too large
- cellophane for lining the box
- floral foam, both dry and wet
- thin plastic film

METHOD

1 Prepare your box by lining with cellophane.

2 Wrap the foam that has not been soaked in thin plastic film so it does not absorb water. Place at the bottom of the box. This will make it much lighter to carry. Place wet foam on top of sufficient depth to take the stems. The foam should be snug in the box and about 2.5cm (1in) below the rim of box.

3 Cut the flowers short and insert in the foam, angled slightly over the rim.

4 Fill in any gaps with small-leaved foliage.

EXPERT TIP

- Flowers with short or bent stems are referred to as 'seconds' in the trade and are therefore less expensive. They are ideal for this design as only very short stems are required.

FLOWERS FOR THE TABLE

Flowers on the table create the focus and beauty that are both essential.
Am I biased – of course not!

The usual shape for tables at more formal weddings is round, seating eight to ten people. Rectangular tables that can be linked end to end are also popular, particularly for the more casual wedding.

RIGHT AND FAR RIGHT
A table centrepiece of *Alchemilla mollis* (lady's mantle), *Ammi* (Queen Anne's lace), *Eustoma grandiflorum* 'Alissa White' (lisianthus), green and white *Hydrangea* and a mix of beautiful fragrant roses including *Rosa* 'White O'Hara' and spray *Rosa* 'White Bombastic', with *Bupleurum* and *Pittosporum*.
Designer: Judith Blacklock

Design for a round table

Getting the right height for the table arrangements is important. Too high and the guests cannot see over them (unless the flowers are raised). Too low and there is no impact and the flowers are lost amongst the menu card, wine cooler and the other paraphernalia on the table. It is said that a table arrangement should be a maximum of 28cm (11in) high but today I prefer a maximum of 35cm (14in).

Step-by-step

Level of difficulty

Mechanics and sundries ★

Arranging ★★

Flowers and foliage

- outline foliage such as *Eucalyptus*, *Gaultheria* (salal), *Hedera helix* (ivy), *Ligustrum* (privet), *Ribes* (flowering currant) or *Ruscus hypoglossum* (hard ruscus)
- 7–9 round leaves such as *Hedera* (ivy), *Galax*, *Heuchera* or *Pelargonium* (optional)
- 6–9 round flowers such as bloom *Chrysanthemum*, *Dahlia*, bloom *Dianthus* (carnation), mini *Gerbera*, *Helianthus* (sunflower) or *Rosa*
- spray flowers or berries such as *Alstroemeria*, spray *Chrysanthemum*, spray *Dianthus*, *Gypsophila* (baby's breath), *Hypericum* (St. John's wort) or *Viburnum tinus*

Mechanics and sundries

- container about 12–15cm (5–6in) in diameter and height
- refuse sack (optional)
- a third to half a brick of foam
- pot tape (optional)

METHOD

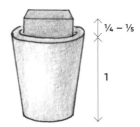

1 Soak the foam for 40–60 seconds, depending on size, then place it in the container. If your container is porous line it with a piece of plastic sheet cut from a refuse sack. As a rough guideline the foam should rise a quarter to a fifth of the height of the container above the rim. If the container tapers towards the base you may simply be able to wedge in the foam so that it is secure. If not, use pot tape over the top of the foam and down the two sides of the container. Pinch the tape between the fingers so that the tape takes less space over the foam. Allow room around the foam for water to be added.

(a)

2 Place a stem of foliage centrally in the foam, in position (a). This should be the height of the container plus half the height of the foam above the rim. Once you have placed the stem in the foam, it will be about the same height as the container. There is frequently a temptation to have the stem longer, but if it is much longer it will upset the proportions of the finished design.

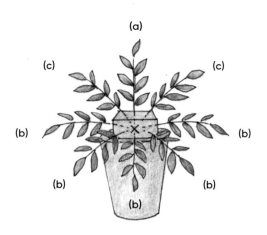

3   Place stems in position (b). These will be the same length as (a). The first few times you create this design use the same type of foliage for all the placements to make it easier to get a regular shape. Insert stems just above the rim of the container, angled slightly downwards over the container. This is very important: if the stems are angled too sharply downwards they will appear to be falling out; if they are placed slightly upwards the flowers and container will appear as two parts and look awkward. All stems should appear to originate from the area marked X, which is at the centre of the exposed foam. It can be difficult to gauge how many stems to use, but as a rough guideline use sufficient stems for the leaves closest to the foam to almost touch the ones next to it.

4   At the top of the foam, place stems (c), which should be the same length as (a). Put them in between rather than directly above the material you have already inserted. They should all appear to come from area X. The overall form of your arrangement will be a gentle dome, wider at the base than the top. There should be more or less equal space between each stem of foliage.

5   If you have round leaves, add them now. They are not essential but do give additional interest and a smooth texture. If they are difficult to find, create a stronger shape with more outline foliage. At this point you will be able to see a small amount of foam but it should not be obvious.

6   Position your round flowers through the foliage outline. Your first flower placement should reinforce the central stem and be upright. If it is angled away from this central vertical position, it will be difficult to achieve a symmetrical design. Try not to go beyond the outline created by your foliage. Again, all stems should appear to radiate from area X.

7   Add your other flowers and berries to complete. If they are light and airy, such as *Chamelaucium* (waxflower), *Clematis*, *Gypsophila* (baby's breath) or *Solidago* (golden rod) you can go a little beyond the established framework without upsetting the balance or proportions.

8   Remove any pot tape from the sides of the container that can be seen.

9   Ensure that your container always has a reservoir of water.

RIGHT A simple placement of summer flowers placed in water in a rectangular glass container suitable for a long table. The flowers in the design are *Astilbe* 'Europa', *Rosa* 'Dancing Cloud', *R.* 'Lovely Dolomiti' and *Veronica* 'Fountain' with *Asparagus densiflorus*, *Eucalyptus parviflora*, *Grevillea*, *Rosmarinus* and *Rubus*.
Designer: Tomasz Koson

FOLLOWING PAGE

▼ A table centre piece using *Aesculus parviflora*, *Amaranthus caudatus*, *Bupleurum*, *Camellia japonica*, *Celosia argentea*, *Cymbidium*, *Echeveria derenbergii*, *Eustoma grandiflorum* 'Alissa Green', *Gerbera* 'Rosata', *Gloriosa* 'Leonella', *Leucospermum* 'Tango', *Lonicera*, *Paeonia* 'Coral Charm', *Papaver somniferum*, *Pelargonium*, *Rosa* 'Rene Goscinny', *R.* 'Suzy Q', *Tulipa* 'Apricot Parrot' and *Viburnum*.
Designer: Elizabeth Hemphill

Designs for a rectangular table

A rectangular table lends itself to designs that follows its long form. The flowers could be a continuous length or in shorter lengths interspersed with items such as candalabra, lanterns, candles and menus.

Long and low

This design is quick and easy to make, but it does need a relatively large amount of plant material. It can be easily adapted for a window ledge or mantelpiece.

ABOVE Long shallow trays filled with foam created a design to run the length of a rectangular table. The flowers used were *Chrysanthemum* 'Aljonka', *Dianthus* (carnation), *Eryngium* (sea holly), *Eustoma* (lisianthus), *Hydrangea*, *Hypericum* 'Coco Casino' (St. John's wort) and spray *Rosa*, with *Gaultheria* (salal), *Pittosporum* and *Skimmia japonica*.

Designer: Judith Blacklock

LEFT This base for this long and low design was a garland of long-lasting foliage purchased from a wholesaler, although you could easily make one yourself. The garland was placed along the table and decorated with plastic tubes filled with *Paeonia* and *Rosa* 'Quicksand', with *Kochia*. The flowers were transported to the event in cardboard boxes covered in chicken wire which supported the tubes.
**Designer:
Elizabeth Hemphill**

RIGHT Table designs of *Freesia*, *Hydrangea*, *Phalaenopsis*, *Rosa* and *Syringa* (lilac). The repetition of the low tables, the candles, the accessories and of course the flowers leads the eye rhythmically to a shimmering flower wall featured at the end of the line.
**Designer:
Abdulaziz Alnoman**

BELOW AND RIGHT Mini hand-ties were placed to follow the curve of the top table which was a demi-circle. Larger versions were placed at strategic points through the venue.

Designer: Judith Blacklock

PAGE 132 ▶ Louise Roots, head florist at Leeds Castle, created this impressive design in the dining room for a private wedding. She used David Austin *Rosa* 'Juliet', *R.* 'Miranda' and *R.* 'Tess' combined with *Rosa* 'Quicksand' and *R.* 'Black Bacarra' from Colombia. These mirrored the flowers seen in the tapestries which are a special feature of Leeds Castle. She added seasonal flowers, including *Astrantia*, *Astilbe*, *Cosmos atrosanguineus* 'Chocolate' and *Dahlia*, together with *Cymbidium* 'Charlie Brown', which picked up the colour of the antique plates around the room. The flowers were displayed in glass vases grouped together at a low height for the guests to see over easily.

Designer: Louise Roots

Tall raised designs

This elegant, eye-catching design can be created in several ways in a variety of raised containers, but it is essential that the stem is slender so as not to obscure people's view across the table, so one made of glass is ideal. The design can be used in the centre of a round table or at suitable intervals along a long table. Flowers can be placed at the base or this space can be used for food at a buffet reception.

Step-by-step

Level of difficulty
Mechanics and sundries ★★
Arranging ★★

Flowers and foliage
- line foliage with a natural curve such as *Danae racemosa* (soft ruscus) or *Eucalyptus*
- plain smooth leaves such as *Hedera helix* (ivy), *Hosta* or *Parthenocissus tricuspidata* (Boston ivy)
- line/spray flowers such as *Clematis*, *Dendrobium* (Singapore orchid), *Eustoma* (lisianthus), or *Symphoricarpos* (snowberry)
- round flowers such as mini *Gerbera*, small *Hydrangea* or open *Rosa*
- other spray flowers of choice such as *Aster*, *Hypericum* (St. John's wort) or *Solidago* (golden rod)

Mechanics and sundries
- container 70–90cm (30–36in) tall
- florists fix and floral adhesive (optional)
- 25cm (10in) posy pad with a polystyrene base, a third of a brick of floral foam, wire hairpins/lengths of strong stems or sticks, florist's fix (optional)

or

- floral foam and a tapered dish or bowl that fits securely in the container's opening, foam holder (frog) and florist's fix and/or pot tape

LEFT To create these sumptuous table centrepieces, extravagant plumes of ostrich feathers were combined with *Dendrobium*, *Hydrangea* and *Rosa*, together with pearls and crystals, and placed in foam-filled clear plastic dishes in the top of tall, glass vases.

Designer: Khalida Bharmal

METHOD

1 Fill the container with water to give ballast.

2 If you are using the posy pad place this, polystyrene side downwards, on top of the container and press so that the opening indents the foam. The pad will now fit securely on top of the container. If additional security is needed, place florist's fix around the rim of the container. Wet the pad.

3 Now take a third of a brick of wet foam and attach it to the centre of the posy pad. For extra security you can glue the two parts together with floral adhesive, push stems vertically through the foam and pad or join the two parts with long wire hair pins. A combination of these methods can be used.

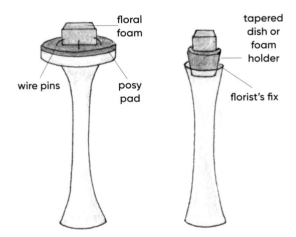

floral foam

tapered dish or foam holder

wire pins

posy pad

florist's fix

4 If you are using a tapered dish adhere a foam holder to the base with florist's fix. Place a piece of soaked foam on the holder. Add tape if you wish. For additional security you may want to put florist's fix round the rim of the tall container. Make sure the dish is concealed by plant material angled downwards.

5 Now that you have your chosen mechanics in place, position a stem of line foliage centrally in the top of the foam (a). Take further lengths of foliage (b) and angle them downwards out of the sides. These should be of different lengths to add interest. Do not angle the stems so sharply that they appear to be falling out or insufficiently so that the arrangement seems to be perched on the container.

6 Take additional stems (c) and angle them out of the top of the foam to make a stronger, fuller shape with your line foliage. At this point there should be a uniform distance between each stem.

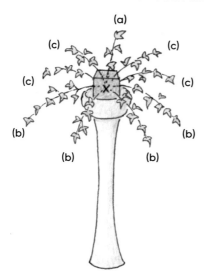

7 Add some plain, smooth leaves for contrast and interest. Adding these fills out the shape inexpensively and gives textural contrast.

8 Reinforce the foliage outline with flowers which have flexibility or a curve in their stems, such as *Dendrobium* (Singapore orchid) or *Eustoma* (lisianthus). Slightly curving stems are easier to work with than rigid stems. Place the first flower stem centrally (this will only be short). Continue placing other flowers throughout the design.

9 Add the round flowers.

10 Fill in with spray flowers and any additional foliage.

Variations

● Add a posy ring at the base and cover with flowers and foliage as for the ring for hanging (see page 46). It is important to have the ring in position before you start to decorate it.

● Stand the design on a circle of mirror glass and add votive candle holders around the base of the stand, perhaps linked with petals or small vases using flowers in the main design.

● For a buffet table where there is no concern about blocking a view, fill the vase with fruit or vegetables, shells, aggregate, coloured water or a swirl of long-lasting grass such as *Schoenus melanostacys* (flexi-grass) or *Xanthorrhoea australis* (steel grass).

RIGHT A tall, slim glass vase, with a posy pad and square of foam at the top, was used here. The outline structure was created with *Danae racemosa*, *Eucalyptus cinerea*, *E. parviflora*, *Hedera helix* 'Arborescens' (tree ivy) and *Skimmia japonica*. *Dianthus* (carnation), *Eustoma grandiflorum* 'Double Green' (lisianthus), *Rosa* 'Peach Avalanche' and *R.* 'Red Naomi' were then added. Small vase arrangements, using the same flowers as in the top placement, were arranged on a mirror base.
Designer: Judith Blacklock

LEFT Tall designs were required on either side of the table reserved for the ceremony. Three glass vases containing *Cornus* (dogwood) were grouped together. Stems also continued the line out of the top of the taller vases, complemented by a mass of tulips.

Designer:
Dawn Jennings

RIGHT Elizabeth Hemphill attached a clear plastic disc to a candelabra with a central plate, having first removed its arms. Flowers and foliage used were *Aesculus parviflora*, *Amaranthus caudatus*, *Bupleurum*, *Celosia argentea* var. cristata, *Cymbidium*, *Echeveria derenbergii*, *Eustoma grandiflorum* 'Alissa Green', *Gerbera* 'Rosata', *Gloriosa* 'Leonella', *Leucospermum* 'Tango', *Lonicera*, *Paeonia* 'Coral Charm', *Papaver somniferum*, *Pelargonium*, *Rosa* 'Rene Goscinny', *R.* 'Suzy Q', *Tulipa* 'Apricot Parrot' and *Viburnum opulus* 'Roseum' with *Camellia japonica*.

Designer:
Elizabeth Hemphill

Tall raised design with a candle

This is a quick and easy alternative to the previous design and is suitable where space is at a premium and there is only a small budget for flowers. The design could be repeated down a long stretch of rectangular tables. A great advantage is that it gives maximum impact without taking up a great deal of space.

Step-by-step

Level of difficulty

Mechanics and sundries ★★

Arranging ★★

Flowers and foliage

- line foliage with a natural curve such as *Hedera helix* (ivy) or *Eucalyptus*
- round leaves (if available)
- round flowers
- spray flowers

Mechanics and sundries

- plastic candle holder for a taper candle or cocktail/kebab sticks and pot tape
- candle
- floral foam
- bottle or candlestick
- candle cup or dish with a cork glued to the base

METHOD

1 If you are using a candle holder place the candle in the holder. Alternatively, place four or five cocktail sticks/pieces of kebab stick on a length of pot tape. The tips of the cocktail sticks should rise just above the tape to give security but not be too obvious. Wrap the tape around the candle so that the edge is on a level with the base of the candle. Instead of sticks you could use lengths of thick florist's wire bent into hairpins.

2 Place the candle cup, or small container with a cork at the base, in the bottle or candlestick. Add soaked foam. Position the candle in the centre of the foam.

3 Place a stem of foliage vertically as close to the candle as possible – it should not be more than half the height of the candle.

4 Follow the same method as for the tall, raised design.

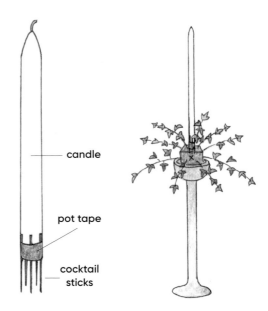

candle

pot tape

cocktail sticks

5 Add leaves with a contrasting texture to reinforce the outline.

6 Position your flowers through the design. The more dominant round flowers should be placed around the central area of the design. Keep checking that you have colour both at the top and at the bottom of the design.

RIGHT Specially designed holders along the front row of the church contained candle cups filled with *Alchemilla mollis* (lady's mantle), *Eustoma grandiflorum* 'Alissa White' (lisianthus), *Rosa* 'White O'Hara' and *Thlaspi* 'Green Bell'.

Designer Mo Duffill

Candelabrum

Candelabra come in lots of different shapes and forms. This method is suitable for a one with four arms and a central protrusion. This particular candelabrum is 1m (3ft 3in) tall and the distance between each arm is 50cm (20in). A design in a candelabrum is most impressive – not the easiest to create but not as difficult as it looks.

Step-by-step

Level of difficulty

Mechanics and sundries ★★/★★★
Arranging ★★

Flowers and foliage

- flexible linear foliage such as *Danae racemosa* (soft ruscus) or *Eucalyptus*
- large, smooth leaves such as *Bergenia*, large *Hedera helix* (ivy), *Heuchera* or small *Hosta*
- additional foliage with contrasting form and texture
- round flowers such as mini *Gerbera* or *Rosa*
- spray flowers ideally with a flexible stem such as *Eustoma* (lisianthus)

Mechanics and sundries

- cloth or towel
- 1m (3ft 3in) candelabrum with four arms and a central protrusion
- 2 pieces of 60cm (24in) chicken wire 5cm (2in) gauge
- 4 bricks of foam
- cable ties

RIGHT The mechanics for this design were two foam rings, with a polystyrene base, placed in the centre of the candelabrum so that the foam was top and bottom. The plant material used was *Alchemilla mollis* (lady's mantle), *Ammi* (Queen Anne's lace), *Hydrangea*, *Rosa* 'White O'Hara' and spray *Rosa* 'White Bombastic', with *Danae racemosa* (soft ruscus) and *Eucalyptus cinerea*.

Designer: Judith Blacklock

METHOD

1 Place the cloth or towel under the candelabrum to catch water drips.

2 Cut a piece of chicken wire sufficiently large to wrap around the foam. Wet the foam bricks.

3 Ask a friend to hold two bricks vertically either side of the central protrusion. Squeeze the foam firmly to fit between the arms and be up against the central protrusion. Wrap the chicken wire around and secure with cable ties. Trim the ends.

4 Take the two remaining bricks and repeat on the other two sides. Cut off the sharp angles of the foam.

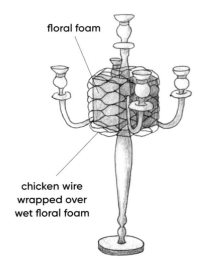

floral foam

chicken wire
wrapped over
wet floral foam

5 Starting with the foliage, place a stem centrally.

6 Place flexible stems out of the central area of the foam so they arch gently. To give an idea of length, they should be about half the height of the candelabrum if pulled straight.

7 Take more stems to create a loose round shape by placing them so they appear to come from the centre of the foam.

8 Add stems of contrasting foliage.

9 Position a flower centrally.

10 Position your larger round flowers in the area about halfway down the design.

11 Fill in with your remaining plant material.

BELOW A contemporary candelabra with contemporary decoration.
Designer: Kate Scholefield

Variations

- Use a sphere as your mechanic and cover with flowers and no foliage to create a compact ball of flowers.
- Add a ring of flowers or several small vases of flowers at the base.

RIGHT A candle cup containing foam was placed in each of the openings of the candelabrum. Candles supported with tape and barbecue sticks were then inserted in the centre of the foam. The plant material included *Callicarpa* and *Eustoma grandiflorum* 'Double Lavender' and *E g.* 'Double Green' (lisianthus), with *Eucalyptus parviflora*, *Heuchera*, *Lavendula*, *Pittosporum, P. tenuifolium* 'Variegatum' and red and green *Skimmia japonica*.
Designer: Judith Blacklock

Inside the container

These ideas are quick, easy and inexpensive to make and have a wow factor.

ABOVE A single flower can create a centrepiece large enough for a table of eight. The rose here was impaled on a pin holder, the base of which was covered with a strip of *Aspidistra*. The design was completed with a swirl of *Schoenus melanostachys* (flexi-grass).

Designer: Tomasz Koson

LEFT Wedding flowers on a budget. A single head of *Hydrangea* was cut short and placed on a pin holder, the pins hidden with smooth pebbles from the beach. An *Aspidistra* and *Dypsis lutescens* (yellow cane palm) were added low down to frame the flower.

Designer: Judith Blacklock

RIGHT Coils were created with decorative aluminium wire. The *Hydrangea* was then cut short and placed through the coils which gave support. Ferns were swirled round the fish bowl to give additional interest.

Designer: Judith Blacklock

LEDGES

Long, straight, narrow ledges are suitable for a wide range of designs.
You could use a collection of vases but here are some other ideas.

Parallel design

This design is perfect when space is at a premium, but you do need height as the plant material rises vertically from the foam with only a minimal amount of radiation. It is surprisingly elegant when multiple placements are created to make a run down the centre of a long table, providing space either side.

LEFT Two parallel designs with the same plant material of *Astrantia*, *Campanula*, *Consolida* (larkspur), *Dianthus barbatus* 'Green Trick', *Eustoma grandiflorum* 'Rosita Double Purple', spray *Rosa*, *Scabiosa* 'Raspberry Scoop' and *Trachelium* arranged in a loose garden style. Rhythm flows through the two placements by the wrapped *Aspidistra* at the base and the flow of colour, form and texture. Variation in the two designs placed 'end to end' gave added interest. Further placements could be added to run the full length of the table or ledge.

Designers: Sarah Hills-Ingyon and Karen Prendergast

Step-by-step

Level of difficulty

Mechanics and sundries ★
Arranging ★★

Flowers and foliage

- mix of linear and round flowers such as *Allium*, *Delphinium*, small *Helianthus* (sunflower) and *Liatris* that can be staggered in height to give overall vertical movement
- round flowers if your vertical placements are linear to give focus at the base
- short stems of foliage for the base
- smooth-textured single leaves for the base
- fruit and/or vegetables, sisal stones, reindeer moss or flat moss (optional)

Mechanics and sundries

- low tray and floral foam or a Medi or Maxi OASIS® Deco
- pot tape

METHOD

1 If you cannot find OASIS® Deco you can use a rectangular florist's tray instead. Cut it in half lengthways with scissors (not as difficult as you would think), slot the two lengths together so they overlap and glue to create one narrow container.

2 Cut foam to fit and soak it, then place in the container. The foam should be higher than the container so that you can angle plant material over the rim. Tape in place.

3 Create the vertical placements with linear plant material. For a container about 25cm (10in) long, three verticals will look effective. If the container is longer you could use four, five or more – there is no limit. The height of the tallest verticals should be greater than the width of the finished design. Position the other placements slightly in from the ends to ensure good balance. The verticals can be bunched or simply graduated down in height. Most stems will have their own point of origin and will not radiate from a central core, although some radiation is needed to create a less rigid design.

4 If you wish, add further shorter vertical placements of round flowers such as *Dianthus* (carnation) or *Helianthus* (sunflower). These will give focal dominance and interest at the core of the design. Keep them low and relatively central, as the strength of their form could otherwise upset the overall balance of the design.

5 Cover any foam that is still visible with short plant material in groups or blocks of contrasting form, texture and colour. If available, include smooth-textured plant material such as *Aspidistra*, *Hedera helix* (ivy) and *Fatsia*. You could clip or manipulate them to fit the space and add interest.

6 You may wish to add flowers such as spray *Chrysanthemum* or *Limonium* (statice) that can be broken down into short units to bring colour to the base of the design. Alternatively, you could add fruit and vegetables, stones, reindeer moss or flat moss to give interest and cut down on cost.

RIGHT A parallel design at the foot of the pulpit using *Chrysanthemum* 'Anastasia', *Eustoma*, *Gladiolus* and *Lilium longiflorum* on a base of *Euonymus* and other mixed foliage. The spray trays at the base were raised with plastic boxes.
Designer: Susan Marshall

Curved flowing design for top tables, ledges and mantelpieces

This front-facing design has a low triangular shape with flowing plant material. It is ideal for the top table, and also mantelpieces and ledges, including lecterns and the lychgate outside the church which often has a ledge. The perfect container is a long, low florist's tray which will be hidden.

ABOVE *Alstroemeria*, *Chamelaucium* (waxflower), *Dahlia*, *Echinops ritro*, mini *Gerbera* 'Picture Perfect', *Rosa* 'Blueberry', *R.* 'Miss Piggy' and *R.* 'Tacazzi' and *Scabiosa*, complemented by immaculate *Hosta* leaves, *Hedera helix* (ivy), fine twigs and *Lavendula* heads, were arranged in two long plastic trays filled with shallow foam – just perfect for a low ledge or centre of a table.

Designer: Kath Egan

FOLLOWING PAGE ▶ Two trays each containing three bricks of foam were placed centrally on this massive mantlepiece. Long stems were inserted into the sides of the foam, to extend the design and drape over the edges. Flowers used were *Eustoma grandiflorum*, 'Alissa Pink', *Paeonia* 'Sarah Bernhardt', *P.* 'Coral Charm' and *P.* 'Coral Sunset', spray *Rosa* 'Lady Bombastic', *R.* 'Sofia Lauren', *R.* 'Karenza', *R.* 'Bubblegum', and *R.* 'Lady Margaret' with *Danae racemosa* (soft ruscus), *Eucalyptus cinerea*, *Hedera helix* (ivy) and *Asparagus densiflorus* 'Myersii' (foxtail fern). A flat top to the design repeated the lines of the coving and picture frame.

Designers: Judith Blacklock and Tomasz Koson

Step-by-step

Level of difficulty

Mechanics and sundries ★

Arranging ★★

Flowers and foliage

- flowing foliage such as *Danae racemosa* (soft ruscus), *Eucalyptus* or *Hedera helix* (ivy) trails
- additional foliage with contrasting form and texture
- linear, round and spray flowers

Mechanics and sundries

- long, low tray
- floral foam
- pot tape

METHOD

1 Fill the tray with wet foam. You can take pot tape around the foam for additional security.

2 Place a stem of foliage (a) in the centre of the foam, two-thirds of the way back and angled slightly backwards.

3 Add further stems to each end of the foam at the length required (b), curved down over the edge of the ledge. You now have the triangle ABC.

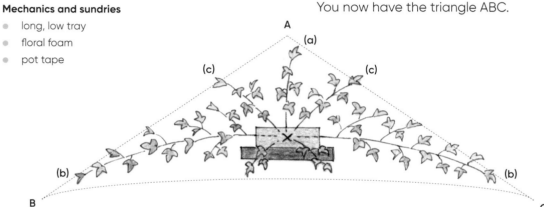

ABOVE A long, low design suitable for a ledge or the centre of a long table. Blues and purples are popular colours for weddings and during the summer months these are easier to source. Here there are *Aster*, *Eustoma* (lisianthus), *Gentiana* and *Hydrangea* on a base of *Eucalyptus cinerea* and *Rumohra adiantiformis* syn. *Arachniodes* (leather leaf fern).

Designer: Judith Blacklock

4 Take more stems out of the top of the foam (c) to fill in the triangle ABC. All the foliage should appear to radiate from the centre of the foam (X). The triangular form ABC will have a curved base.

5 Incorporate contrasting foliage to add strength and interest to the outline.

6 Place a flower in the top centre of the design. Position other flowers so they reinforce the outline by taking colour through to the points (a), (b) and (c) and then through the design.

7 Position one dominant round flower two-thirds of the way down from the tallest stem and the remainder at regular intervals through the design.

8 Fill in with flowers and foliage of choice.

> ### EXPERT TIP
> - Add fruit on cocktail or kebab sticks or wired conifer cones to give inexpensive form and texture.

RIGHT A long, low florist's tray was placed in the centre of a ledge at the top of the lychgate. *Fagus* (beech) and *Hedera helix* (ivy) created the outline. *Hydrangea*, *Lilium*, *Rosa*, spray *Rosa* and *Thlaspi* 'Green Bell' made this an impressive entrance to the church.

Designer: Judith Blacklock

FOLLOWING PAGE ▶ In this exuberant mantelpiece design by Amanda Austin Flowers, a base of *Fagus* (beech) was decorated with *Chamelaucium* (waxflower), *Dahlia*, *Hydrangea* and *Rosa*.

Designer: Amanda Austin Flowers

BELOW *Alchemilla mollis* (lady's mantle), *Antirrhinum*, *Hydrangea arborescens* 'Annabelle', *Phlox* and *Rosa* arranged in an OASIS® Medi Deco, decorated the ledge on the lectern.

Designer: Mo Duffill

CAKE DECORATION

The wedding cake will be an important centrepiece at the reception and it is frequently decorated with fresh flowers. Flowers can be used in many ways to enhance the creativity and design of the cake but you will need to take the following points into consideration, liaising with the bride and the cake designer at all times.

THE WEDDING CAKE - PLANNING AHEAD

- If you have time visit the venue. Take a camera/phone for reference images.

- Check the shape, diameter and depth of the cake after it has been iced and the shape of the table on which it is to be presented. It is always best to have a round cake on a round table and a square cake on a square table.

- Telephone the reception venue to confirm that the cake table will be in the required position. This should not be close to a radiator or in front of a fire or emergency exit sign. Just think of the pictures!

- Find out when the cake is arriving and make sure you have enough time to arrange fresh flowers.

- Ask if the cake is to be seen in the round or only at the front and sides.

- Check whether the cake is a sponge or a fruitcake so you know how robust it will be.

- Check whether the cake has been professionally made or bought from a supermarket. If the latter, you might have a pile of boxes to unpack and dispose of.

- Ask whether the layers will be separated and, if so, with what.

- If the cake is chocolate or 'naked' do not set up until immediately before the wedding reception as this type of cake deteriorates quickly in the heat and may attract insects.

- If the cake is iced, an ivory icing suits warm colours such as peaches and yellows and a white icing suits blues and pinks.

- Find out if the flowers you use should repeat those in the bride's bouquet.

- Bring spare flowers and petals to decorate.

- Prepare the topper (top-tier arrangement) beforehand and finish in situ.

- Ask if the cake-maker can supply extra sugar paste, which can be used to fix flowers in place. Alternatively, there is an edible cake glue that can be used.

- If the cake is unstructured, with little or no decoration, keep the floral additions in the same vein.

- If using ribbon disguise the join with a bow or perhaps a flower.

- Cover or hide the cake boards.

- Make sure no wires are showing.

LEFT A beautiful cake featuring the famous flamingos, popular residents of the Roof Gardens Restaurant in London's Kensington. A scattering of tulip petals was all that was needed to show it to advantage. They also served to discourage small hands from playing with the sugar-paste flamingos.

Design ideas

- A stacked cake could have a corsage at different points (see page 212).

- Flowers could be displayed in a small vase on the cake itself.

- Loose flowers can be threaded through the cake and on the table. Use flowers that will last without water for several hours.

- Decorate an OASIS® Iglu Floral Foam Mini Deco holder.

- If you use pillars, glass or acrylic vases to separate the layers of the cake, make sure there is a board underneath the bottom layer to give strength.

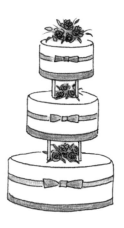

- If you use polystyrene spacers between tiers you will need to hide all the polystyrene with flowers and/or foliage.

- Wire ivy trails very loosely so they can be draped around the cake.

- Surround the cake with a ring of flower petals. Not only does this look pretty but it also creates a barrier and may stop small children touching the cake.

- Suggest that the bride and bridesmaids put their bouquets on the table by the cake.

RIGHT Bloom *Chrysanthemum*, *Erica* (heather) and *Rosa* 'Sweet Avalanche' have been placed on the different tiers of the cake. Care was taken so that the flowers were not in direct contact with the icing.

Cake designer: Crème Velvet

Decorating the wedding cake

This simple but effective round design is perfect for the top tier of a wedding cake. The container should be small. Lids from aerosol cans are perfect, but they need to be put through the dishwasher first to remove any potentially harmful residues. However, if the bride wants a slender container it may be necessary to wire the flowers in a posy-style construction so that the wired stem can be inserted into the container. This will take longer to construct than this design, which is made in floral foam.

Step-by-step

Level of difficulty
Mechanics and sundries ★
Arranging ★

Flowers and foliage
- short *Hedera helix* (ivy) trails, perhaps cut from a pot plant, or other small-scale foliage
- round flowers such as individual heads of spray *Rosa*
- filler flowers and foliage

Mechanics and sundries
- aerosol can top
- floral foam
- pot tape
- disc of cellophane or fabric

METHOD

1 Thoroughly wash the aerosol can top. Cut a small piece of foam to fit, allowing a small amount of foam to sit above the top. Soak the foam.

2 Secure the foam using pot tape if necessary.

3 Place the first stem of ivy in the centre to establish the height. Insert further stems about 10cm (4in) long into the sides of the foam, at a slight downwards angle so they cascade over the edge of the container.

4 Place a rose or flower of your choice centrally in the foam. This should also be about 10cm (4in) tall.

5 Position the remaining flowers through the design just below the central position. Radiate all stems from the centre of the visible foam.

6 Fill in the shape you have created by adding further stems of foliage and flowers, all within the outline you have established.

7 Lightly spray and store in a cool place until required on the cake. Have a suitably sized disc of cellophane or fabric to place on the cake prior to adding the container.

RIGHT A three-tier cake, with layers 30, 23 and 15cm (12, 9 and 6in) in diameter, covered in sugar paste. Lengths of dowelling were placed between the layers to stop them sinking into each other. The cake was decorated with *Chamelaucium* (waxflower), *Freesia*, *Rosa* and spray *Rosa*. A 20cm (8in) OASIS® posy pad was placed beneath the cake, with a mirror on top to stop the cake board getting soggy. Flowers were also inserted sideways out of the posy pad.

Designer: Angela Veronica

The bouquets carried by the bride and bridesmaids will probably be the most photographed flowers on the day, so every detail needs to be perfect. Wiring is an integral part of creating wonderful displays for the entire bridal party. If stems are not wired, flowers and foliage may wilt, trailing flowers from a semi-wired bouquet may drop out as the bride walks up the aisle and corsages may fall to pieces.

This section covers the basics of wiring, followed by step-by-step instructions on how to create buttonholes and flowers for the hair, before moving on to bouquets for the bride and designs for the bridesmaids.

FLOWERS FOR
THE BRIDAL PARTY

PLANNING AHEAD

Expert tips on choosing flowers and foliage

- Flowers in season will be stronger, last longer and cost less.

- Fresh flowers should have firm green foliage with no yellowing.

- The pollen from lilies stains badly so it is best to avoid using this flower in bouquets for the bride and bridesmaids. Even if you have removed the stamens from the open flowers other blooms will open. If a bride adores lilies and makes a special request, advise her not to rub or wash off any pollen but to remove it with sticky tape. Just gently dab the pollen and most of it should lift off. While this does not guarantee total removal it should make any spots less obvious. Hanging the article on a clothes line on a sunny day should help remove the last touches.

- I love the smell of lilies but there are many who do not, so do check.

- Ask if the bride and bridesmaids have any allergies. Some flowers such as *Solidago* (golden rod) and *Eremurus* (foxtail lily) can cause severe sneezing. Not what you would wish for in the middle of the service!

- Avoid using *Euphorbia* as this causes severe eye and skin irritation, especially in sunlight, and *Aconitum* (monkshood), which is very poisonous.

- Herbs are lovely in summer bouquets. My favourites are *Mentha* (mint), which will last a surprisingly long time when mature, *Origanum* (marjoram) and lemon-scented *Pelargonium*. *Rosmarinus* (rosemary), which has pretty blue flowers several times a year, is always available.

- Choose flowers and foliage that are mature and robust for wired designs or situations where there will be only a small amount of foam or water to keep them going.

RIGHT The bride carries a hand-tied bouquet of *Astilbe* 'Washington', *Delphinium* 'Delphi's Starlight', *Eustoma grandiflorum* 'Alissa Pink' (lisianthus), *Helleborus* 'Magnificent Bells', *Lathyrus odoratus* (sweet pea), *Nigella damescena* 'Oxford Blue', *Paeonia lactiflora* 'Sarah Bernhardt', *Rosa* 'Pink O'Hara', *Spiraea nipponica* 'Snowmound' and *Viburnum opulus* 'Roseum'.
Designer: Dennis Kneepkens

THE BASICS OF WIRING

If you are only planning to arrange flowers for the ceremony or reception
it is not necessary to learn these techniques, but wiring can
be therapeutic and enjoyable once the basics have been mastered.
It's a skill that will give you confidence and a sense of professionalism.
Your family and friends will be delighted with your efforts.

There are many different methods of wiring and no one way is correct. It can often feel like trial and error, as there are many different flowers of different sizes. As you progress and feel more confident, you will instinctively choose the right weight of wire by feel rather than by number. You will develop your own variations on the techniques, which is great. What's important is that you neither under- nor over- wire. You need to be able to choose the minimum weight of wire for your purpose and this will come with experience. When I first learned wiring, many years ago, I found the instructions difficult to understand. This is why I have given as much detail as possible in the step-by-step designs that follow.

So, what exactly is the purpose of wiring? Wiring enables you to:

- anchor the stems to a base such as the foam in a wedding bouquet holder;

- control the stems so they can be angled in any position;

- extend the length of the stems to give flexibility;

- reduce the weight of the flowers by removing the heavier stems and inserting the lighter wire, making them easier to wear or to hold.

This simple cross-section of a rose shows the various parts of a flower to help understand the various wiring techniques that follow.

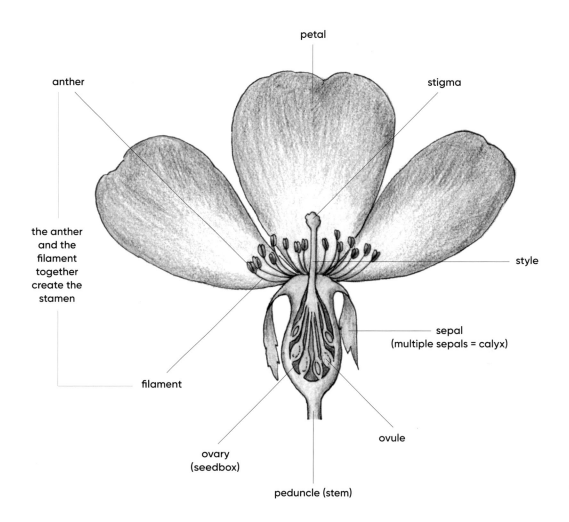

petal

anther

stigma

the anther and the filament together create the stamen

style

sepal (multiple sepals = calyx)

filament

ovule

ovary (seedbox)

peduncle (stem)

ABOVE Cross-section of a flower

Stub wires

Stub wires are pre-cut lengths of wire sold in bundles. They can be black (actually blue annealed) or green plastic-coated. The latter are cleaner to use but more expensive and slightly thicker.

There are many different gauges of wire and choosing the right one can be daunting when starting out. The wires mentioned below are the essentials and need to be sourced if you are serious about creating flowers for the bridal party.

Wires are available in lengths from 18cm to 46cm (7–18in). Perhaps the most useful is 30cm (12in). The gauge or thickness varies from 0.23mm to 1.80mm. The higher the gauge number the thicker and consequently the heavier the wire, so 1.80mm is much heavier than 0.23mm. Very light wires are silver-coloured and called silver wires/silver rose wires/rose wires.

You can buy florist's wires online and if you buy flowers regularly and order wholesale you will be able to order wires with your flowers.

It is essential to remember that the heavier the flower the heavier the gauge of wire you will need.

The most useful gauges, starting with the lightest, are:

- 0.28mm (silver wire) – very fine
- 0.32mm (silver wire) – very fine
- 0.38mm – fine
- 0.46mm – fine
- 0.56mm – medium
- 0.71mm – medium-heavy
- 0.90mm – heavy

And if you wish to narrow these down to five, the following are arguably the most useful:

- 0.32mm
- 0.46mm
- 0.56mm
- 0.71mm
- 0.90mm

They are the ones I have used in this book.

EXPERT TIPS

- It is possible to use two light wires together to make a heavier one.
- It is useful to have the heavier-gauge wires in both medium and long lengths.

Reel wire

Reel wire (also known as binding wire) is purchased on small reels, as the name indicates. It is used to bind items together. It can be black, silver or green plastic-coated. Different gauges are available from 0.28mm to 0.56mm. As with stub wire, the higher the gauge number the heavier the wire, so 0.56mm is for heavier stems and 0.28mm for lighter stems. Reel wire can be cut into lengths if so wished.

The most useful gauges when purchasing reel wire are:

- 0.32mm (silver) – for fine wedding work
- 0.56mm (black or green) – for garlands and heavier design work

Decorative metallic reel wire, which is available in a wide range of colours, is usually left uncovered to become part of the design.

Note
From this point onwards the 'mm' following the wire gauge will be omitted.

ABOVE Once you have perfected your wiring skills and the semi-wired bouquet why not create your own unique bouquet? The beautiful design above was handcrafted from delicate silver wire and embellished with hundreds of Swarovski crystals and beads. White *Dendrobium*, *Freesia*, *Gypsophila* (baby's breath) and silver *Brunia* were used to enhance the transparent, airy feel of this bouquet, which was exceptionally light and easy to carry.

Designer: Sharon Bainbridge-Clayton

EXPERT TIPS FOR USING WIRE

- Cut the wire angled downwards, pointing it away from you, so that it does not jump up and become a potential health and safety issue.

- Use the finest wire possible that will give control without making the plant material rigid and inflexible. Practice and experience will show which gauge of wire is suitable for a particular flower. In order to judge, hold the wire at the end furthest from the flower or a short way up. If it does not bend under the weight of the flower you have the right wire to provide support. Obviously in certain situations it is possible to use a lighter gauge if you are wiring a number of items together or to a base or frame.

- When wiring flowers and leaves, wire ends often get bent, especially when stitching a leaf or inserting the wire through the stem or calyx. It is best to cut off the bent end and start again.

- All wiring must be discreet unless for decorative purposes.

- Do not twist the wires around each other but keep them straight, wherever possible, to ensure a cleaner finish.

- Work on white folded tissue paper so that all the wires can be easily seen and are therefore easier to work with. Coloured tissue can mark the flowers.

- Fine and medium gauges (up to 0.71) can usually be cut using a good pair of flower scissors. Always cut with the thickest part of the blades: that is, the part nearest the handle. For thicker/heavier gauges of wire a wire cutter is best, to prevent damage to scissors or secateurs.

- Sharpen the wire by cutting across the end at a blunt angle.

- Insert the minimum amount of wire into the stem or seed box to minimise moisture loss through transpiration. The more holes you make and the larger the holes, the more easily moisture can be lost.

Using stem tape

Stem tape enables water to stay in the stem longer and not evaporate. It also covers the wires and gives a neat finish.

Which wire, which flower, which technique?

Stems that are used short have to be treated differently from those that are kept longer.

I have recommended certain wires for each technique, but this is purely a guide. You can go a gauge lighter or heavier without any problem.

ABOVE Xin He holds a delicate wired posy of *Hydrangea*, *Jasminum*, *Nigella damascena* (love-in-a-mist), white *Paeonia* and spray *Rosa*. Skeletonised leaves enhanced the look of the flowers and matched the texture of the dress.

Designer: Rebecca Zhang

SUPPORT WIRING TECHNIQUES

For longer stems and to make them flexible

These are often used for larger-scale work, including shower bouquets.

The following specific techniques are used when the stems need to be:

- extended with wire to give a longer length (single- and double-leg mounts);

- secured in place, as in a semi-wired shower bouquet where the wire end is looped over the cage and into the foam (single- and double-leg mounts);

- flexible and with more strength (winding);

- strengthened and the angle of the flower head adjusted (external winding).

Note

The stems are kept longer in the single- and double-leg mount techniques described on the following pages and the wires are often stronger as they have to give greater support because of the length.

FAR RIGHT The outline of the semi-wired bouquet was created with *Danae racemosa* (soft ruscus), then *Chamelaucium* (waxflower), *Eustoma* (lisianthus), *Hypericum* (St. John's wort) and *Rosa* were added.
Designer: Yajie Cao

WIRING TECHNIQUES FOR ORCHIDS

The interesting shapes of orchid blooms require different techniques.

Phalaenopsis

RECOMMENDED WIRE 0.32

METHOD

1 Cut the stem to 2.5cm (1in).

2 Bend a 0.32 silver wire gently so that one end is slightly longer than the other. Thread the two ends through the two small holes at each side of the column at the base of the three petals which constitute the flower. Because the stem is quite soft and susceptible to being crushed when handled, you may find it helpful to insert a fine wire inside the length of stem before bringing the other wires down and taping.

3 Bring the wires down and wrap one around the stem and the second wire so they are equal.

4 Cut the wires to a suitable length and tape (see page 196).

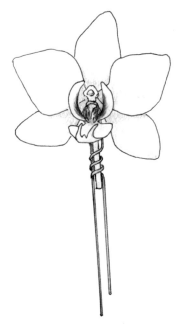

Wiring: *Phalaenopsis*

Cymbidium

RECOMMENDED WIRES 0.71 or 0.90 and 0.32

METHOD

1 Cut the stem to about 2.5cm (1in).

2 Take a 0.71 or 0.90 wire up through the stem.

3 Thread a 0.32 silver wire through the base of the throat. This will keep the flower intact.

4 Bring two equal lengths of the wire down between the petals so they are parallel with the first wire.

5 Cut to a suitable length and tape (see page 196).

Dendrobium (individual flower)

RECOMMENDED WIRE 0.32

METHOD

1 Cut the stem to about 2.5cm (1in).

2 Take a light 0.32 silver wire through the green calax where the stem joins the flower. This keeps the 'throat' intact.

3 Bring the wire ends down so they are parallel with the stem. As with the *Phalaenopsis*, you may wish to insert a fine wire inside the length of the stem before wiring and taping.

4 Bring one wire leg around the natural stem, binding in the other wire(s), keeping them straight.

5 Cut to an appropriate length.

6 Tape (see page 196).

Wiring: *Cymbidium*

Wiring: *Dendrobium*

EXPERT TIP

● Once wired and taped it is best not to spray *Cymbidium* with water as the flowers can mark.

BOUTONNIÈRES, BUTTONHOLES AND CORSAGES

Flowers are an important part of the wedding day for other members of the bridal party as well as the bride. So, what distinguishes a boutonnière, a buttonhole and a corsage?

Boutonniére

The *Concise Oxford English Dictionary* defines boutonnière as 'a spray of flowers worn in a buttonhole'. Some florists say that it is an American word for buttonhole. However, I think the best description is a mini posy of flowers and foliage to be worn, with no one flower particularly dominant. They can be wired or unwired.

Buttonhole

Traditionally worn by the men in the bridal party, a buttonhole is composed of one bold flower complemented by three leaves. Today, embellishments and other plant material are included, but the principal flower retains its dominance.

Corsage

The classic corsage differs from the buttonhole in that it contains a number of the same dominant flower but the scale is smaller: for example, spray *Rosa* rather than *Rosa*. It is usually quite intricate. All the elements are wired.

EXPERT TIPS

- All boutonnières, buttonholes and corsages should be as light as possible so use the lowest-gauge wires that will give support.

- They should be sufficiently robust to stand up to a good hug without being flattened or destroyed.

- Take care to select materials that will tolerate being out of water for several hours.

- Avoid using deciduous leaves early in the growing season as they do not have the strength to stay turgid when cut. They tend to be a brighter, lime-green colour.

RIGHT Joe wears a creative buttonhole of *Amaranthus*, *Hydrangea* and *Rosa* 'Victorian Dream' with *Asparagus setaceus* (lace fern) and *Skimmia*, finished with silk ribbon. All the flowers were selected to match those in the bride's bouquet which Joe is carrying, with an emphasis on the delicate details inspired by nature.
Designer: Kate Scholefield

Boutonnière

An unwired boutonnière is a natural and charming arrangement of a number of flower heads, buds, foliage and berries worn on a dress or jacket. It should give the impression of being freshly picked. It will not, however, last as long as its wired and taped counterpart.

Boutonnières are relatively easy to create. You need to use flowers in season that are well conditioned, relatively robust and with foliage that is mature. Mid- to late summer and autumn are the ideal seasons for creating these. If the stems are not wired, the natural stems form part of the design. Various embellishments such as beads and decorative wire can be added.

Boutonnières can be worn by either men or women, but men traditionally wear flowers on the left-hand side of their jacket and women on the right-hand side of their jacket or dress.

RIGHT Spray *Rosa*, with *Hypericum* (St. John's wort) threaded on *Schoenus melanostacys* (flexi-grass).
Designer: Judith Blacklock

Step-by-step

Level of difficulty

Mechanics and sundries ★

Arranging ★

Flowers and foliage

- *Aster* (September flower), *Astrantia, Chamelaucium* (waxflower), spray *Chrysanthemum, Craspedia* (Billy buttons), *Dianthus barbatus* (sweet William), *Erica, Eustoma* (lisianthus), *Freesia, Hypericum* (St. John's wort), small to medium *Rosa*, spray *Rosa* or *Solidago* (golden rod)
- *Brachyglottis* syn. *Senecio, Eucalyptus, Hebe* or *Rosmarinus*

Mechanics and sundries

- stem tape
- bindwire, raffia, twine, ribbon, wool or lace
- glue

ABOVE AND FOLLOWING PAGE ▶ Unwired *boutonnières* of mixed plant material bound together and named for members of the bridal party.

Designer: Lynn Dallas

METHOD

1 Select small-scale flowers and strong foliage such as *Hebe* or *Rosmarinus* that complement the theme of the wedding or event.

2 Clean and remove the leaves from the bottom part of the stems to prevent the buttonhole becoming too bulky. Condition well by giving the stems a good drink of water immediately prior to arranging.

3 Bunch short lengths of foliage in the hand and add flowers of choice.

4 Bind all the flowers and foliage together with stem tape, leaving the stem ends open.

5 Cut the stems neatly across the bottom. Mist and place in water.

6 Just before delivery or collection, cover the stem tape with bindwire, raffia, twine, ribbon, wool or lace. Tie, adding a drop of glue under the tie for greater security.

ABOVE LEFT Spray *Rosa* with *Pittosporum tenuifolium* 'Variegatum'.

ABOVE RIGHT *Astrantia,* spray *Rosa* with *Hedera helix* (ivy) and *Pittosporum.*

RIGHT *Astrantia, Bouvardia,* with *Pittosporum* and *Betula* (birch) twigs.

Designers: Flower School students

LEFT Should this be called a boutonnière or a buttonhole? Here the terms merge. It's up to you to decide! *Ranunculus* are gorgeous but they need to be sprayed regularly if the weather is warm.

Designer: Judith Blacklock

Buttonhole

Traditionally buttonholes are worn by the groom, best man and men within the bridal party.

As mentioned, a classic buttonhole is composed of one dominant flower such as a *Dianthus* (carnation) or *Rosa* and three leaves. In the past these were usually leaves from a rose, when used with a rose, but today more robust leaves are frequently brought into play such as *Galax*, *Hedera helix* (ivy) or *Ruscus hypoglossum* (hard ruscus). Smaller flowers and berries can be added for interest, but they should be limited and subsidiary to the main flower.

ABOVE *Anemone* is the dominant flower, supported by a spray of *Hypericum* berries, twigs and a swirl of bullion wire.
Designer: Flower School student

ABOVE Individual *Hydrangea* florets were glued onto a cardboard ring. The colour graduated from pale to dark pink and was accented with a single trail of *Muehlenbeckia* vine for a soft, delicate look. Two magnets held the buttonhole in place. If using magnets do check that your designs will not be worn by anyone with a pacemaker, which can be adversely affected.
Designer: Sharon Bainbridge-Clayton

RIGHT Here delicate beads and fine silver wire were included to continue the theme. *Rosa* 'Avalanche' is the dominant flower, arranged with *Asparagus umbellatus* (ming fern), variegated *Pittosporum* and white *Symphoricarpos* (snowberry).
Designer: Sharon Bainbridge-Clayton

Step-by-step

Level of difficulty

Mechanics and sundries ★★

Arranging ★★

Flowers and foliage

- 1 medium-sized *Rosa* (if the rose is too large it will be heavy and be difficult to wear)
- 3 *Hedera helix* (ivy) leaves

Alternative flowers and foliage

- a round flower such as a *Dianthus* (carnation) or mini *Gerbera*
- 3 small *Galax* or *Heuchera* leaves

Mechanics and sundries

- 0.71 wire
- 0.32 or 0.46 wires
- stem tape
- florist's pin or pearl-headed pin

METHOD

1   Cut the *Rosa* or flower of your choice short, leaving 2.5cm (1in) of stem.

2   Insert a 0.71 wire up the stem until you hit a natural resistance.

3   If you are using a rose you can cut 3–5 short hairpins of 0.32 silver wire and insert these through the sepals to prevent the rose from blowing (see page 181).

4   For extra security take one or two 0.32 or 0.46 wires at right angles through the top of the seed box. Fold the wire(s) down.

5   Take stem tape round the seed box and down the 2.5cm (1in) of natural stem, then continue down the wires.

RIGHT A classic buttonhole of a single rose framed by three *Hedera helix* (ivy) leaves.

Designer: Judith Blacklock

6 Using 0.32 wires, wire and tape three leaves (see page 194).

7 Arrange the flower and leaves together in the hand so that the leaves frame but do not obscure or dominate the flower. You could position a leaf behind the flower but I prefer to place them at the sides and towards the front so that it is easier to pin the buttonhole to a dress or suit. But do what works best for you. Position the leaves as high as possible up the seed box of the rose but not above. Manipulate the leaves to make the buttonhole more sympathetic.

8 Cut the wires to a length of 5cm (2in) or the length of three fingers placed sideways. Take the stem tape and wrap tightly round all the wires and the short stem of the flower and leaves to form one single stem. Take the tape back up the stem so that the end is hidden under the leaves and is completely sealed, with no bare wires showing.

9 To present the buttonhole, place it on tissue paper in a box. White tissue is best as coloured tissue can often bleed and stain the flowers resting on it. Lightly mist with water and attach a pin. Cover with cellophane or tissue paper and place somewhere cool until required.

EXPERT TIPS

- Although *Zantedeschia* (calla) is a popular flower for buttonholes and corsages avoid using large ones as they can be particularly difficult to keep upright. *Zantedeschia* 'Crystal Blush' is small and a good choice. For the same reason choose a medium not a large rose.

- Flowers and foliage can be chosen for a special theme such as *Eryngium* (sea holly) for a Scottish wedding or a white rose to represent Yorkshire.

Decorative additions

You can add many different items to make your buttonhole exciting and different: for example, twigs, beads, buttons, diamanté, crystals or small squares of bark. Lots of flower sundry suppliers have many items ready-wired. You could add any small decorative material with a hole in it, such as a pearl, to coordinate with the colour and style of your design.

Here are a few ideas to make your buttonhole look more distinctive. Some of these can also be included in a boutonnière.

Metallic wire curls
Take a pencil and wind decorative metallic reel wire around in a colour of your choice to form a coil with a straight end. Slide this off the pencil and incorporate in the buttonhole with tape. For a smaller coil use a cocktail or kebab stick.

Curling the stem
Wind the stem of the buttonhole around a pencil. Thread a pearl onto the curly end of the stem. Add a drop of glue to ensure that it does not fall off.

***Hypericum* (St. John's wort) berries threaded on *Xerophyllum tenax* (bear grass) or *Schoenus melanostachys* (flexi-grass)**
Cut one end of a stem of bear or flexi-grass at an angle. Thread *Hypericum* (St. John's wort) berries, with or without their calyces intact, onto the grass at suitable intervals. Wire each end with a single-leg mount (see page 184) and tape the two ends together to create loops of the appropriate size.

ABOVE The groom frequently has a buttonhole that is more elaborate than those of the other men in the bridal party and that mirrors the flowers and design of the bride's bouquet. The flowers used here are the same as those in the wedding bouquet on pages 108–109.

RIGHT *Rosa* 'Red Naomi' and white *Hyacinthus* florets, with *Hedera helix* (ivy) leaves and *Salix* (pussy willow).

Designers: Flower School students

ABOVE *Rosa* 'Avalanche' with a surround and wrap around the stems of *Hedera helix* (ivy) bound with silver bullion wire.

BELOW *Cymbidium,* with dark-red *Eustoma* (lisianthus), two short strands of *Xerophyllum tenax* (bear grass) and a single *Galax*.

Designers: Flower School students

ABOVE An elegant red-rose buttonhole, embellished with red *Tasmannia lanceolata* (pepper berries) and trailing *Xerophyllum tenax* (bear grass). The stem was bound with fine gold wire, threaded with tiny red and gold beads to echo the colours. It was attached with magnets to prevent any damage to the suit fabric. If using magnets do check that your designs will not be worn by anyone with a pacemaker, which can be adversely affected.

Designer: Sharon Bainbridge-Clayton

Corsage

Corsages are worn by the mothers of the bride and groom and other important female family members. They are usually attached to a coat or suit lapel or a dress but can be easily adapted for the wrist or handbag. As with all wired designs, care should be taken to select materials that will tolerate being out of water for several hours. Corsages should be as light as possible and therefore the thinnest wires possible should be used. They are usually worn with two-thirds of the stem facing downwards and one-third upwards. Gravity dictates that this is where they sit best and are most visually pleasing, plus there is no wobble!

BELOW For this corsage spray *Dianthus* (spray carnation) was the feature flower.
Designer: Neil Bain

ABOVE AND LEFT In this corsage three *Cymbidium* orchid heads are perfect with a touch of *Alchemilla mollis* (lady's mantle).

Designer: Dawn Jennings

Step-by-step

Level of difficulty
Mechanics and sundries ★
Arranging ★★★

Flowers and foliage
- 6 open spray *Rosa*, small *Rosa* or *Dendrobium* orchid heads
- half-stem of *Chamelaucium* (waxflower), *Dianthus barbatus* (sweet William) or *Hypericum* (St. John's wort)
- 7–9 small *Galax*, small to medium *Hedera helix* (ivy) or any other small to medium round leaves

Mechanics and sundries
- stem tape
- 0.32, 0.46 or 0.56 wires according to the weight of your flowers
- pin, T-bar or magnet for attachment

METHOD

1 Wire the open spray roses, small roses or *Dendrobium*. Tape.

2 Wire about six small bunches of spray flowers using the single-leg mount technique (see page 184).

3 Wire and tape the *Galax* or *Hedera helix* (ivy) leaves.

4 Now start to compose the corsage. The objective is to create a triangular design. Lay the main flowers (in this design the rose) on the table in the shape of the finished corsage. You will want the smallest flower at the top, the largest in the central area and the others in-between.

5 Intersperse the leaves and spray flowers between the roses to make a pleasing display.

6 At this point you will not be using stem tape to add in each stem but you may wish to take a little bit of tape and wrap it round the stems when a few are in place to make your placements more secure.

7 Finish with a leaf or two and a couple of buds placed back to front so that when they are bent back they will come down over the front of the corsage to hide the wired stem. This is called the return end.

8 Now tape the wires downwards where they all come together.

Corsage: main flowers in position

EXPERT TIP
- You can add small wired loops of *Xerophyllum tenax* (bear grass) or *Schoenus melanostacys* (flexi-grass) if you wish. A tiny bow from narrow ribbon can complete the corsage.

EXPERT TIP

- Other flowers that would work are *Dendrobium* (Singapore orchid), spray *Chrysanthemum* or any flowers with a round form. Complement these flowers with those that will survive well without a direct source of water.

BELOW A corsage composed of spray *Rosa* 'A–lady', purple *Callicarpa* and *Hypericum* (St. John's wort) berries, with *Hedera helix* (ivy) leaves.

Designer: Neil Bain

ATTACHING A BOUTONNIÈRE, BUTTONHOLE OR CORSAGE

The boutonnière and buttonhole should be placed so that the flower is pointing upwards. If you are using a pearl-headed pin take it through the fabric, pin through the back and catch the side of the stem. You may need two pins.

Wear a corsage as high up as possible. It is traditional to have the tip of the corsage facing downwards as it is then unlikely to swing around. If you are using a pearl-headed pin take it through the dress or suit material, through the wires of the corsage and back into the clothing.

If you are using a T-bar (which is small, clear plastic and T-shaped) place it vertically down the back of the buttonhole or corsage main stem. You need to use tape to bind around the T-bar and corsage to secure. If the T-bar is longer than the corsage, remove the end of the T-bar with scissors. The pin section should be horizontal so it is easy to attach to clothing.

You can buy magnets the size of a small coin that come in two parts. Glue or tape the thicker part to the back of the main stem of the buttonhole or corsage. Try to place it as high up as possible so it is hidden. The thinner part is then placed inside the clothing, with the buttonhole or corsage on the other side of fabric so that the magnets stick together. Magnets only work well if the clothing fabric is not thick as otherwise they are not sufficiently strong to keep the flowers securely in place. For a very lightweight or delicate fabric such as fine silk or organza a magnet may be the best option as pinning can pull threads or make a hole. Take care with delicate fabric when using wire accents.

Warning

If the person wearing a boutonnière, buttonhole or corsage has a pacemaker, magnets MUST NOT be used as they will interfere with the pacemaker and could cause harm.

LEFT A corsage with flowers from the garden and half a stem of spray *Rosa* from the florist. Here Dawn has used *Bupleurum*, spray *Chrysanthemum* and three *Rudbeckia* (cone flower) as the principal flower with *Cotinus* (smoke bush) and *Quercus* (oak).

Designer: Dawn Jennings

Wrist corsage

Here I describe two quick and simple ways to make a wrist corsage. Start with these and if you enjoy making them you can then go on to experiment with other methods.

Using ribbon

Ribbon adds texture, colour and contrast and can turn a simple buttonhole or corsage into something eminently wearable.

Step-by-step

Level of difficulty
Mechanics and sundries ★
Arranging ★

Flowers and foliage
- broad flat leaves (either the whole leaf or sections) such as *Galax* or *Hedera helix* (ivy)
- 1 or 2 heads of *Phalaenopsis* (taken from a plant or cut stem)
- leaves and flowers of choice

Alternative flowers
- large-headed spray *Rosa*
- *Cymbidium* orchids

Mechanics and sundries
- 2 x 60cm (20in) lengths of 5cm (2in) satin ribbon (sufficient to take round the wrist and make a pleasing bow)
- florist's cold glue
- beads and coils of wire (optional)

METHOD

1 Angle the lengths of ribbon over each other (like a St. Andrew's cross). Use florist's cold glue to secure together in the centre. Whenever you use florist's glue allow time for it to get tacky before adhering ribbon, leaves or flowers.

2 Glue flat leaves to the central part of the ribbon. This creates an easy platform on which you can adhere your flowers and foliage.

3 Cut the larger, flatter flower(s) short so they have virtually no stem. Keep a longer stem on the smaller flowers so they can be tucked in between. Add a touch of florist's cold glue to both the back of the flower and the leaves. Allow the glue to get tacky and adhere the two together. Hold for a few seconds so they are secure. You can work from the outside edges to the centre or from the centre outwards – your choice!

4 Glue on additional flowers, foliage and extras such as beads and coils of wire.

5 Remove any trails of glue.

6 The corsage may then be placed around the wrist and the two ribbon ends tied in a neat bow.

EXPERT TIPS
- When gluing *Cymbidium* cut the stems and leave them to air-dry so that the sap at the end of the stem seals.
- For very delicate materials use a cocktail stick to apply the glue.
- Try on at intervals to check shape and balance.
- Recess some of the plant material to allow for movement, but do not make the focal material too high as the design must be easy to wear.

Base for ribbon wrist corsage using *Hedera helix* (ivy) leaves

BELOW This wrist corsage was based on 7.5cm (3in) ribbon pleated towards the two ends and bound to reduce the visual weight. A single *Phalaenopsis* was used, with *Ceropegia*, *Eucalyptus cinerea*, *Muehlenbeckia*, *Senecio* 'beads' and *Stachys byzantina* (lamb's ear). Magnets were added to the underside of the ribbon and concealed with *Eucalyptus* leaves. This also makes it easier to separate the magnets.

Designer: Sarah Hills-Ingyon

Using a ready-made corsage bracelet

A corsage bracelet with a central disc for the addition of flowers provides a base for a quick and easy assemblage of flowers and foliage.

ABOVE This design, based on a Corsage Creations bracelet, features *Bouvardia*, *Eustoma* (lisianthus), mini *Gerbera* and *Hypericum* (St. John's wort), with *Xerophyllum tenax* (bear grass).

Designer: Mo Duffill

Step-by-step

Level of difficulty

Mechanics and sundries ★
Arranging ★

Flowers and foliage

- broad flat leaves (either the whole leaf or sections) such as *Aspidistra, Galax* or *Hedera helix* (ivy)
- heads of *Phalaenopsis* (these can be taken from a plant)
- berries, leaves and flowers of choice

Alternative flowers

- *Anthurium*
- *Cymbidium* orchid
- *Gerbera*
- mini *Gerbera*

Mechanics and sundries

- florist's cold glue
- ready-made wrist corsage bracelet. We used one from Corsage Creations.

METHOD

1 Dab glue on the plastic disc and allow it to get tacky.

2 Using the disc as the base follow the same method on page 218.

EXPERT TIPS FOR USING GLUE

- Specialist cold glue works better than hot glue as the latter can burn and discolour delicate floral materials.
- Make sure the flowers are dry before gluing.
- Use pliers to squeeze the nozzle of the tube to an oval to control the flow.
- Pour a little glue onto a smooth surface and allow to get tacky before applying.
- Cut the flowers as short as possible to give the widest surface area.
- Glue adheres best when touching more glue, so spread it carefully on both surfaces to be placed together.
- Avoid handling the glued item for about 10 minutes after placing the flowers.
- If you lose the cap to your glue tube insert a pin with a large head. When you finish a tube keep the cap.

FLOWERS FOR THE HAIR

Flowers for the hair can be very simple and easy to create such as combs and headbands. Circlets and crowns are more intricate in their creation and a few trial attempts before the day are needed to ensure success.

Comb

This delightful, quick and easy way of decorating the hair involves no wiring. Two widths of comb are commonly available: 7.5cm (3in) and 10cm (4in).

LEFT AND RIGHT Combs with matching plant material of *Astrantia*, *Nigella damascena* (love-in-a-mist) and spray *Rosa* on a base of *Eucalyptus* leaves. The petals of *Nigella* drop quickly but the seed heads left behind are charming.
Designer: Judith Blacklock

ABOVE A single bold *Anthurium*, with *Danae racemosa* (soft ruscus), knotted *Liriope* (China grass) and *Muehlenbeckia*. Sarah worked from the outside to the centre, placing the *Anthurium* last. A blade of *Liriope* was added to the back of the comb to hide the mechanics.

Designer: Sarah Hills-Ingyon

ABOVE Red spray *Rosa* and *Eustoma grandiflorum* (lisianthus), with a loop and tail of *Schoenus melanostachys* (flexi-grass) and a flourish of beads threaded on bullion wire, on a *Hedera helix* (ivy) and *Quercus* (oak) leaf base.

BELOW View from the back.

Designer: Sarah Hills-Ingyon

ABOVE Dennis used an alternative decoration for the hair. He simply covered the stems of the plant material with wet cotton wool, which was then wired and taped. The wiring meant that the flowers could be securely attached to the hair using hairclips.

Designer: Dennis Kneepkens

RIGHT Megan wears a floral headpiece featuring *Hydrangea*, *Eustoma* (lisianthus), *Rosa* 'Victorian Dream', spray *Rosa* 'Jana' with *Asparagus* foliage and pepper berries. The flowers are designed to sit to one side of the head so they do not appear to be too heavy.

Designer: Kate Scholefield

ABOVE A long-lasting, fresh-flower hairpiece using one spray *Rosa* 'Lovely Lydia', together with spray *Chrysanthemum* 'Ibis', flowers from a single stem of *Ornithogalum thyrsoides* (chincherinchee) and strands of *Xerophyllum tenax* (bear grass) on a base of *Eucalyptus*. Floral glue keeps the plant material in place. A swirl of textured ribbon completes the design.

Designer: Sarah Hills-Ingyon

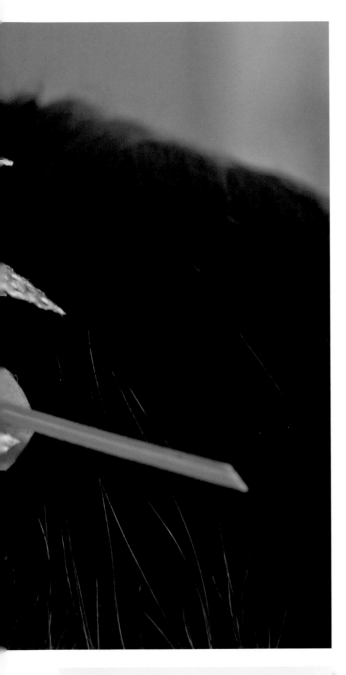

Step-by-step

Level of difficulty

Mechanics and sundries ★

Arranging ★

Flowers and foliage

- small to medium smooth-textured leaves such as *Eucalyptus* or *Hedera helix* (ivy)
- small to medium flowers, berries and foliage

Mechanics and sundries

- florist's cold glue
- florist's comb

METHOD

1 Take a layer of glue along the top of the comb. Allow the glue to get tacky, which will take a couple of minutes.

2 Glue a foundation of smooth-textured leaves along the top of the comb. Overlap them slightly and take over the edges of the comb, but leave the teeth mostly uncovered.

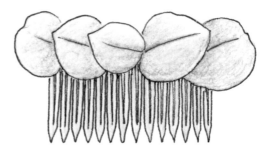

Base for comb using *Eucalyptus* leaves

EXPERT TIP

- The comb could also be decorated with a small wired corsage or spray of delicate flowers glued in place as a single unit.

3 Lay out the flowers and foliage in the pattern you wish to use. You will want overlapping layers to give depth and interest.

4 Finish with a round flower at or close to the centre.

Headband

Headbands are charming for young bridesmaids but also look lovely on those of other ages. They are much quicker and easier to make than floral circlets. Plain plastic, fabric or metal headbands are the best to use as the flowers and leaves can simply be glued on. The glue acts in a similar way to stem tape, sealing in the moisture and reducing water loss. Make sure the headband fits the head for which it is intended.

Step-by-step

Level of difficulty
Mechanics and sundries ★
Arranging ★

Flowers and foliage
- small plain leaves such as *Hedera helix* (ivy)
- small to medium round flowers such as spray *Rosa*, small orchid heads or *Clematis*
- filler flowers and berries such as *Chamelaucium* (waxflower), *Hypericum* (St. John's wort) or *Gypsophila* (baby's breath)

Mechanics and sundries
- florist's cold glue
- headband
- about 1.20m (3ft 3in) length of 2.5cm (1in) satin ribbon (optional)

METHOD

1 Place florist's cold glue along the length of the headband and leave for several minutes to get tacky.

2 Start by placing a few small *Hedera helix* (ivy) or other plain leaves on the band so they overlap. Alternatively, cover the headband with ribbon and only place leaves on the central area.

> ### EXPERT TIPS
> - When covering the headband with ribbon first cut two lengths about 5cm (2in) long. Fold a length over each end of the band and glue in place. Tuck any excess at the sides to the back to ensure that there are no exposed raw edges, which could fray. Wrap the remaining ribbon with regular overlaps around the band – about 40 per cent overlap each time – and the two ends already covered in ribbon. Use dabs of glue to keep it tightly in place. Start and finish close to the prepared ends.
> - Use silk flowers for a long-lasting headpiece.

3 Place the more dominant round flowers at regular intervals along the band.

4 Fill in any gaps with filler flowers, berries or leaves.

Headband part-covered with *Hedera helix* (ivy) leaves

ABOVE *Eustoma grandiflorum* 'Rosanne Deep Brown' (lisianthus), *Hypericum* 'Coco Bamboo' (St. John's wort) and spray *Rosa* 'Jana' on a covered headband of *Hedera helix* (ivy) leaves.

Designer: Sarah Hills-Ingyon

Floral circlet

A pretty, feminine design, this classic circular band of flowers is traditionally worn by young bridesmaids but can also be worn by brides. It will take several hours to construct correctly, but what follows is a sure-fire way to create a circlet that will look good throughout the wedding and not fall to pieces as the bride walks up the aisle. I also give details of how to make a quick version if you are in a hurry, but only make this one if it is to be worn by someone less central to the day.

When selecting flowers, remember that a lot of body heat is emitted from the head and that the wired flowers will be out of water for several hours. Care should therefore be taken to select suitable flowers which have been well conditioned. The lasting quality of flowers in a wired design is of the utmost importance. As the flowers will be close to the face, do not incorporate any that are known to contain allergens or are poisonous, such as *Aconitum* (monkshood).

EXPERT TIP

- If you are unsure about the suitability of any fresh material, it is a good idea to do a test run – cut, wire and leave it overnight to see how it fares.

RIGHT The hair circlets on these charming bridesmaids were composed of *Chamelaucium* (waxflower) and *Rosa*, with *Hedera helix* (ivy) leaves.
Designer: Judith Blacklock

FOLLOWING PAGE ▶ A delicate floral circlet using *Gypsophila* (baby's breath), *Hebe* and spray *Rosa*.
Designer: Dawn Jennings

Made to measure

A good fit is essential so it is important to measure the head (with the desired hairstyle in place) before the circlet is made. Take a piece of string around the head to get the measurement. Lie this flat, next to a tape measure, to measure exactly what length you need. Add an extra 6cm (2½in). A circlet that is too large is easier to adapt than one that is too small.

Step-by-step

Level of difficulty
Mechanics and sundries ★
Arranging ★★★

Flowers and foliage

- single round flowers such as the individual roses from about 5 stems of spray *Rosa*, 3 stems of *Dendrobium* or 9 small *Rosa* such as *Rosa* 'Akito' or *R.*'Heaven'
- filler flowers such as 2 stems of *Chamelaucium* (waxflower), 2 stems of *Gypsophila* (baby's breath) or 3 stems of *Solidago* (golden rod)
- small *Hedera helix* (ivy) leaves
- foliage with contrasting textures – the best leaves are those which fill quickly, such as *Asparagus umbellatus* (ming fern) or *Hebe*, but this may not be necessary if you are using filler flowers with fluffy foliage or lime-green material such as *Alchemilla mollis* (lady's mantle)

Mechanics and sundries

- 0.90 wires for the base
- stem tape
- 0.32, 0.46 and 0.56 wires for the flowers and foliage according to weight and form
- 0.32 or 0.46 wires for eyelets (optional)
- satin ribbon (optional)
- sharp fabric scissors (to cut ribbon)

Note
The number of stems listed is a rough guide only, as how many you need will depend on the number and size of the flowers on each stem.

TOP LEFT A circlet of purple and white *Dendrobium* orchids with *Chamelaucium* (waxflower) and *Hedera* (ivy).
Designer: David Thomson

LEFT A doggie circlet is a delightful way of including pets into the celebration. Just ensure that you use no harmful plant material and remember that all parts of the lily are poisonous to cats.
Designer: Judith Blacklock

METHOD

1 Ensure that you have conditioned all plant material well. In warm weather, flowers and foliage taken from the garden should be cut in the cool of the evening or early morning, then immediately placed in water. Purchased flowers should always be re-cut and placed in clean water with flower food for a long drink. Cut the stems on a slant.

2 Prepare the circlet. Tape two long (45cm/18in) 0.90 wires together to make one continuous length. They should overlap by about 7.5cm (3in). If you only have shorter wires you can add in a third 0.90 wire. Cut to the length required and tape. You could use green, white or brown tape depending on the colours of your plant material.

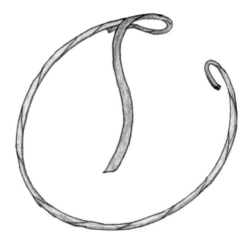

Covering a circlet with stem tape

3 At this point you can place the wire around a round vase to get a smooth circular shape. When using a lot of heavy plant material I prefer to keep the wire straight as it is easier to manipulate.

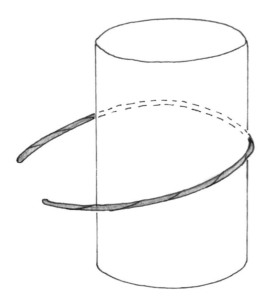

4 At one end of the wire make a hook and at the other end make a small loop (shaped like the eye of a needle). Tape in the loop to secure in place. Together the loop and hook will make the fastening.

5 Wire small bunches of flowers and foliage and single stems by the appropriate method according to weight and form.

6 Once you have wired all the materials, begin taping. If you feel you can work with half the width of the tape, cut it in two. This reduces the bulk but is a bit more difficult to use. Cut the wired and taped flowers and foliage to about 4cm (1½in).

7 Place the first bunch over the loop, then take the tape around the bunch and circular base once or twice to hold it in position. Place a flower or foliage to each side, again taking the tape once or twice around them and the base to secure. Cut off any excess lengths of wire. Work to the top and to the two sides but not the back, as this needs to lie flat against the head. Make sure there are no wires present that might scratch the head.

Adding bunches of flowers

8 Eyelets can be placed at three or four points around the inside of the circlet. These are small loops which can be used as anchor points so that hairgrips can be threaded through to keep the headdress in place. An eyelet is made by taking a 0.32 or 0.46 wire, making a small loop with a tail and then taping the tail firmly into the circular base (optional).

eyelets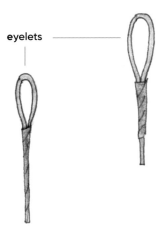

9 Keep a good balance of plant material, mixing textures as you go until you have covered the whole circlet.

10 If you wish to finish the circlet with a bow, make two ribbon loops – like a figure-of-eight – with two tails. Take a short length of wire over the centre of the bow, tape the ends and incorporate into your design.

EXPERT TIPS

- It is quicker to wire all materials first and then tape rather than stopping and starting both jobs.

- A rough guide to scale is to have no flower that is more than twice the size of the next flower, or group of flowers. However, smaller flowers can be grouped to increase the scale.

- If you are unable to take head measurements add ribbon at both ends of the circlet so it can be either tightened or loosened. If you are creating a heavier circlet the ribbon will need to be wider and therefore stronger to support the extra weight. The ribbon chosen should link with the colour of the flowers.

- Remember to keep moving consistently down the wire to ensure that your additions do not get bunched together and thus create a bulky effect. You may also run out of flowers!

- If it makes it easier, snap off the tape and resume whenever you wish.

- You may find it easier to swing the circlet round when you tape as you near completion and that is fine. Alternatively, keep turning it upside down and work from both sides.

Floral circlet: quick and easy method

This circlet is not as secure or as comfortable to wear, but once you are confident with the technique it should work when time is at a premium.

RIGHT AND BELOW A circlet of mini *Cymbidium* and *Eustoma* (lisianthus) with *Viburnum tinus* on decorative aluminium wire.

Designer: Dawn Jennings

Step-by-step

Level of difficulty

Mechanics and sundries ★

Arranging ★★

Flowers and foliage

- a mixture of flowers and foliage – we have used *Astrantia* and *Eustoma* (lisianthus), with *Danae racemosa* (soft ruscus) and *Rosmarinus*

Mechanics and sundries

- 55–60cm (26–28in) of 2mm coloured aluminium wire (see page 314)
- stem tape
- 2 lengths of 1.25 or 2.5cm (½ or 1in) satin ribbon
- dressmaking scissors

METHOD

1   Cut a length of coloured aluminium wire to be the base of the circlet.

2   Create a small loop at each end. Tape over the wire ends using stem tape, leaving the loops open so you can thread the ribbon.

Circlet with aluminium wire base

3   Cut the stems of the flowers and foliage so they are about 2.5cm (1in) long.

4   Lay the flowers and foliage in a pleasing order, starting and finishing with a piece of foliage.

5   Place the first piece of foliage, in this instance *Danae racemosa* (soft ruscus), to just cover the end of one loop and join to the wire with stem tape. Do this twice so that it is secure.

6   Place your first flower over the foliage and tape in.

7   Continue adding flowers along the wire, interspersing foliage at regular intervals. Finish with a piece of foliage.

Adding flowers to aluminium wire

front view   back view

8   Thread a length of ribbon through each of the two loops so that the circlet can be secured. Cut the ends neatly with dressmaking rather than florist's scissors.

EXPERT TIP

- Select plant material with thin stems as this will give a more elegant finished look.

Floral crown

A floral crown is the term for a circle of flowers composed of larger blooms. As a consequence, a crown needs heavier wires, such as 0.71, to support the stems. They look lovely in photographs but are not nearly as practical, as the flowers are heavier and consequently more difficult to secure and wear for a full, active day. If you want to create a floral crown I suggest you work to create the perfect circlet first and then the crown of flowers will follow on more easily.

RIGHT An exuberant floral crown and bouquet of *Allium, Clematis, Rosa* 'Red Naomi' and *R.* 'Harlequin', with *Hedera helix* (ivy) leaves.
Designer: Jo-Anne Hardy, Posy & Wild

BELOW A floral crown of *Dendrobium* (Singapore orchid), *Dianthus* 'Antiqua' (carnation) and *Hydrangea* with *Ruscus hypoglossum* (hard ruscus).
Designer: Neil Bain

PACKING AND PRESENTING WIRED AND GLUED ITEMS

Boutonniéres, buttonholes, corsages, circlets and wedding bouquets can usually be made the day before. Spray tissue paper and the flowers lightly with water or a professional spray such as Chrysal Professional Glory (available online) and then put them in a polythene bag in a cool, not cold, fridge.

If fridge space is limited or unavailable an alternative method of storage is to use a cardboard box such as the type in which flowers are delivered to a wholesaler or florist. Line the box with damp tissue paper, undyed to avoid colour running. Lightly mist the items with water, then place them on the tissue. Cover the box with thin transparent film and seal the edges to retain moisture. Put the box somewhere cool and dark – a tiled or stone floor in a basement would be ideal – unless using exotic flowers that do not like the cold.

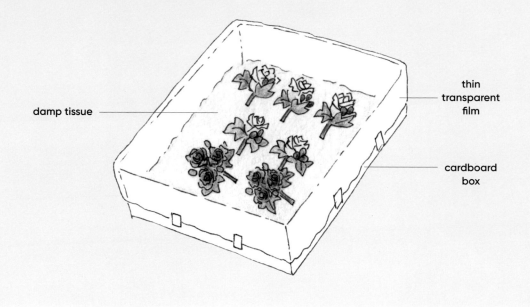

damp tissue

thin transparent film

cardboard box

RIGHT Flowers around the hair using *Alstroemeria*, *Dahlia*, *Freesia* and *Tweedia coerulea* (white star), with red berries.

Designer: Risa Takagi

WEDDING BOUQUETS

The bridal bouquet is perhaps the most important design at any wedding.
Here I describe the three most popular styles today: the hand-tied,
the structured massed and the semi-wired shower bouquet.
Together these comprise the vast majority of bouquets seen at weddings.

ABOVE A Rolls-Royce is of course
the perfect vehicle to show off
this semi-wired bouquet.
Designer: Mo Duffill

RIGHT A bouquet to match the headdress on page 243,
again using *Allium, Clematis, Rosa* 'Red Naomi' and
R. 'Harlequin', with *Hedera helix* (ivy) leaves.
Designer: Jo-Anne Hardy

Hand-tied bouquet

Creating the perfect hand-tied bouquet is easier than you might think. They can be made in more than one way. For example, many commercial florists like to turn and twist as they go, but I prefer the method outlined below, which I find easier.

Learning how to make a hand-tied is rather like riding a bike: once it clicks you wonder why you ever thought it difficult!

LEFT This bride's hand-tied bouquet was designed to create a natural romantic style. *Eustoma* (lisianthus), *Matthiola* (stock) and David Austin *Rosa* 'Juliet' were complemented by *Eucalyptus populus* which gave delicate movement.

Designer: Lauren Murphy

BELOW *Ranunculus* are not the easiest flowers to include in a hand-tied bouquet as their stems are soft and break easily. However, they are incredibly beautiful so do consider working with them once you have mastered the hand-tied.

Designer: Judith Blacklock

Step-by-step

Level of difficulty

Mechanics and sundries ★

Arranging ★★/★★★

**Flowers and foliage:
what to choose and what to avoid**

Choose

- at least one type of round flower such as bloom *Chrysanthemum*, standard *Dianthus* (carnation), mini *Gerbera*, mini *Helianthus* (sunflower), *Paeonia* or *Rosa*
- foliage to add interest and volume and show off the flowers: *Asparagus virgatus* (tree fern), *Cotinus*, *Hedera helix* 'Arborescens' (tree ivy) or *Physocarpus opulifolius* 'Diabolo' would look lovely
- straight stems, as they are easier to work with than those with a bend
- spray forms that add charm and contrast when combined with the round flowers

Avoid

- stems that branch low down. If your chosen stems do, then remove the lower branches. They can always be incorporated into table arrangements, buttonholes or corsages.
- stems that have a defined bend
- flowers that have a volumetric shape, i.e. those that have space within the flower once it has opened such as *Iris* and *Lilium*, as the shape will change dramatically in just a few days
- flowers with soft stems such as *Anemone*, *Ranunculus* and *Zantedeschia* (calla) until you are more experienced
- stems that are tall and linear such as *Gladiolus*, as you will have to remove many of the flowers lower down the stem or they will stick out rather noticeably

Mechanics and sundries

- pot tape or garden twine
- raffia or ribbon
- secateurs

LEFT A hand-tied bouquet of *Astrantia*, *Eustoma* (lisianthus) and *Rosa* 'Avalanche', with seeded *Berzelia lanuginosa* (buttonbush), *Eucalyptus decipiens* (redheart moit) and *Panicum capillare* (witchgrass), with a swirl of gauze.

Designer: Risa Takagi

METHOD

1 Remove the foliage from the bottom two-thirds of the stems. Have a length of pot tape or garden twine and a pair of scissors to hand.

2 If you are right-handed make a spiral of stems as follows (if you are left-handed see the note on page 252):

- Curve your left arm so that the palm of your hand is at the level of and in front of your chest. Hold the first stem vertically in the palm of your left hand at a level so that you can see down into the flowers. Use your thumb to hold the stem secure. Keep your fingers slightly curved and together.

- Cross a second stem over the first. The head of the flower should be pointing towards the shoulder of the hand holding the stems.

- Take a third stem and repeat the action in the same direction. Keep adding foliage to space out the flowers and give bulk. I personally like to alternate the majority of flower placements with a stem of foliage. The heads of the flowers should all be at the same height.

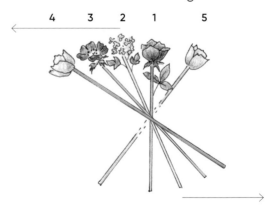

- Continue adding stems, all in the same direction. Keep looking down into the bouquet to check there is a good balance of colour, form and texture.

- From time to time you will need to add a stem in the opposite direction (5). Do NOT do this by crossing a stem in front but by slotting it, at a diagonal cross to the previous placements, between the palm of your hand and the back of the stems already in place. This will make a spiral. You can place stems in this direction at any time. The heads of these stems will be angled towards the shoulder of the hand that adds the flowers.

3   When you have placed the majority of the stems, you may wish to insert a dominant flower at the centre. Do this by gently wiggling a stem through the centre of the bunch so that it is vertically positioned down the middle of the hand-tied.

4   To tie, hold the bunch tightly in your left hand. Double a length of garden twine so that one end is longer than the other. Hold this in your right hand. Take the longer length around the bunch twice, above where it is being held, not below, and pull until you feel tension, without snapping the stems. Take the two ends together and knot or tie in a bow. If using pot tape simply wrap round the stems a few times until secure.

5   You are now ready to cut the stems neatly. I like the width of the bouquet and the height of the stems to be equal. Bring the stems together firmly, low down in one hand, and cut straight across. Do this over a bin to avoid a scattering of stem ends. You will probably need secateurs for this.

6   A simple way to decorate the stems is to cover the binding material with raffia or ribbon.

Note

If you are left-handed, hold the bouquet flowers in your right hand and add them with your left. The technique is the same: you place your stems with the tips pointing towards the shoulder of the hand holding the flowers (right shoulder). The stems behind face the opposite direction. To tie, hold the bunch in your right hand.

EXPERT TIPS

- As you add more stems you may wish to curve or cup your hand slightly to give additional support.
- Hand-tied bouquets are the perfect gift to say thank you to the bride's mother and others who have helped with the wedding.
- As a hand-tied is able to stand unsupported it is a great design to display vertically on the top table at the reception. Tap the cut stems on the table before placing the bouquet there.

RIGHT A bouquet of *Freesia*, *Rosa* 'White O'Hara', spray *Rosa* 'White Bombastic' and *Veronica* with *Eucalyptus cinerea*.
Designer: Judith Blacklock

FOLLOWING PAGE ▶ A hand-tied bouquet of *Astrantia*, *Delphinium*, *Paeonia* and *Veronica* with *Eucalyptus cinerea*.
Designer: Talking Flowers

PREVIOUS PAGE ◄ An asymmetric bouquet created using the spiralled technique. To achieve the cascade, longer pieces of *Danae racemosa* (soft ruscus), *Jasminum* and *Polystichum* were placed to one side. Strong focal flowers anchored the design on the opposite side to balance the longer stems. *Anemone, Astilbe, Astrantia, Brunia, Dahlia, Daucus carota* (wild carrot), *Echeveria, Eucalyptus, Gardenia jasminoides, Jacobaea maritima, Jasminum, Kochia, Lysimachia clethroides, Paeonia, Papaver somniferum, Pelargonium, Polystichum munitum, Protea cynaroides, Ranunculus, Rosa* 'Quicksand', *Scabiosa, Serruria florida* with *Camellia, Danae racemosa* (soft ruscus), *Davallia* (deersfoot fern), *Olea* (olive), *Thlaspi* and *Thryptomene calycina* were used to create this splendid bouquet.

Designer: Elizabeth Hemphill

ABOVE A classic hand-tied bouquet was given a contemporary feel by the addition of a handcrafted beaded collar of Swarovski pearls and beads, designed to mirror elements in the bridal bouquet. *Chrysanthenum* 'Kermit' (santini), *Freesia*, green *Hypericum* (St. John's wort), *Rosa* 'Avalanche' and *Symphoricarpos* (snowberry) created a fresh colour palette.

Designer: Sharon Bainbridge-Clayton

RIGHT AND FOLLOWING PAGE ▶ Alexandra is holding a handtied bouquet that was created using similar flowers that decorated the wedding reception at the Caledonian Club.

Designers: Judith Blacklock and Tomasz Koson

Structured massed bouquet

A mass of beautiful flowers will always look stylish. This bouquet can be created very quickly once you have practised a few times. The flowers keep their natural stems and are surrounded by one or two rings of complementary wired leaves to give a tailored finish. If time is at a premium use sturdy leaves that do not have to be wired.

The number of flowers used will depend on the size of the desired bouquet. If using roses, slightly open blooms are much better than tight buds for this design and those with a flatter rather than pointed appearance look softer and more natural.

LEFT This structured bouquet for a traditional Japanese wedding was created by Tomoyo Fujisawa for Hisako, who is wearing a traditional kimono. Tomoyo used *Chrysanthemum* 'Anastasia', spray *Chrysanthemum, Eustoma* (lisianthus) and *Paeonia*, with *Galax* leaves. The decoration for the stems and a bead rope involved *mizuhiki*, a traditional Japanese art form using cord that is made from starched rice paper not wire. Gold, silver, red and white are auspicious colours in Japan.

Designer: Tomoyo Fujisawa

RIGHT A simple perfect dome of 20 fragrant *Rosa* 'Norma Jean'.

Designer: Jane Maples

LEFT A massed bouquet of *Rosa* 'Vendela' surrounded by two layers of *Galax* leaves.

Designer: Judith Blacklock

Step-by-step

Level of difficulty

Mechanics and sundries ★
Arranging ★★

Flowers and foliage

- 16–20 roses or other flowers of a similar size and form such as *Chrysanthemum*
- 20–30 large *Galax* or *Hedera helix* (ivy) leaves

Mechanics and sundries

- soft cloth
- pot tape
- 0.32 or 0.46 wires
- 1m (3ft 3 in) length of 2.5cm (1in) satin ribbon
- stem tape
- 3 pearl-headed pins
- scissors

METHOD

1   If using roses, gently remove all the leaves and thorns. Check the flower heads for any imperfections. Take a soft cloth and rub along the stems to make sure they are perfectly clean. Remove any damaged or bruised petals, but not too many.

2   Cut three lengths of pot tape and place at the edge of your table for easy access. Choose a well-shaped flower for the centre that is neither too small nor too large. Mass the other flowers together in a gentle dome shape around the central flower. Keep the stems straight, spiralled or semi-spiralled, whichever suits you best. Check the profile of the bouquet from all angles regularly to ensure that the dome is even and round.

3   Take pot tape firmly around the stems about 5–7cm (2–3in) below the bottom of the flower heads. If you take it too high it may snap the stems. Trim a little off the stem ends and place in water.

4 To make a collar of leaves, wire the *Galax* or *Hedera helix* (ivy) leaves using the stitching technique described on page 194. Tape.

5 Create two rings of wired leaves around the flowers. The leaves should overlap. The first ring will have the back of the leaves outwards. They need to sit so that there is a small amount of leaf showing all the way round the outside of the bouquet. Rest your bouquet on the edge of the table and secure the first ring of leaves with pot tape. The second ring will have the front of the leaves outwards and positioned a little lower down to cover the wires of the first ring. Secure this second ring of leaves with stem tape or pot tape (stem tape gives a finer finish).

6 Very carefully cut the wires below the tape, making sure they are long enough to be secure and won't fall out.

7 Take stem tape around the top of the stems, just below the leaves, and down over the wire ends.

8 Cover the stem tape with ribbon to create a handle. Starting just below the leaves, wrap the ribbon round and round down the length of the stems so that each wrap overlays the previous by about 40 per cent. The total width of the ribbon wrap is usually about a hand's width plus two fingers along the handle. The satin side of the ribbon should be facing inwards to the stems.

EXPERT TIPS

- To check if the bouquet is symmetrical and well structured, stand in front of a mirror to assess.

- *Gypsophilia* (baby's breath) could be used instead of roses. The effect is magical but you need a lot of stems and it is more time-consuming to make than using roses.

9 When you have covered the required length of stem, twist the ribbon so that the satin end is now facing outwards. Wind it back to the top immediately below the bottom of the outer leaves. Cut and fold the end over so no frayed edges show. Secure with pearl-headed pins at regular intervals down the handle. Insert the pins at a vertical slant so they do not pierce the other side of the handle.

10 Cut the stems to the appropriate length.

ABOVE Lucy Lu's hand-tied bouquet is composed of *Rosa* 'Juliet', *Hypericum* 'Pinky Flair' (St. John's wort), *Matthiola* (stock), *Paeonia,* spray *Rosa* 'Pink Flair' and *R.* 'Salinero', with *Eucalyptus* and *Jacobaea* (silverleaf).

Designer: Khalida Bharmal

RIGHT A rustic, informal bouquet of Colombian *Hydrangea, Rosa* 'Avalanche' and *R.* 'Sweet Avalanche', with *Brunia,* seeded *Eucalyptus* and grey velvety *Brachyglottis.*

Designer: Jane Maples

LEFT A Turkish bride holding a structured massed bouquet of *Gypsophila* (baby's breath).

Designer: Unknown

RIGHT This round bouquet was created on a foam holder. *Eustoma* (lisianthus), the tiny flowers of *Tweedia coerulea*, *Rosa* and *Pittosporum* were angled out of the foam to create a spherical design.

Designer: Risa Takagi

ABOVE This bouquet was made by keeping the stems tightly aligned to create an elegant, slightly domed design. It combined the strong, deep tones of *Rosa* 'Black Baccara' and *Zantedeschia* (calla), with the fruits of *Viburnum tinus* to give texture and fine detail.

Designer: Lauren Murphy

RIGHT A rich, jewel-toned bridesmaid's bouquet in shades of burgundy, red and deep pink was perfect for an autumnal wedding and looked stunning against the gold of the bridesmaid's dress. The bouquet includes *Astilbe* 'Paul Gaarder', *Cosmos atrosanguineus* 'Black Magic', *Dahlia* 'Black Fox', *Rosa* 'Black Baccara' and spray *Rosa* 'Lady Bombastic'.

Designer: Sharon Bainbridge-Clayton

BELOW A beautiful Carmen rose made from the petals of 12 roses surrounding one beautiful bloom. The design is not detailed in the book but it is sure to give inspiration. The petals can be pinned or glued to the central flower and it is incredibly light to hold. Such a wedding bouquet may be small but is sure to attract attention.

Designer: Neil Bain

RIGHT A shower bouquet of *Cymbidium*, *Eustoma* (lisianthus), *Hypericum* and *Rosa* 'Avalanche' with *Asparagus virgatus* (tree fern) and *Eucalyptus parvifolia*.

Designer: Dawn Jennings

Semi-wired shower bouquet

This design is suitable for a bride who wants a classic bouquet that is timeless anywhere in the world, one that creates glamour and style. It is sometimes called a cascade, waterfall or teardrop bouquet.

The size of the bouquet will depend on the bride's height and the style of her dress. The standard length of a shower bouquet is 60cm (24in), but Princess Diana's bouquet was more than 1m (3ft 3in) in length. The weight must have been considerable.

For a standard-length bouquet, one-third will be 20cm (8in) above the centre (or bullseye) of the holder and two-thirds will be 40cm (16in) below to give good proportions. When making your calculations add on 2.5cm (1in) to the length to cover the amount of stem inserted into the foam which will not be seen.

The overall shape is gently rounded at the top. A good profile can be achieved by ensuring that the materials at the top are slightly angled back over the handle of the bouquet holder. The lower part of the design consists of flowers and foliage which appear to cascade from the central point.

EXPERT TIP

- All longer, lower materials should be wired before inserting into the foam, but the bouquet should still have plenty of natural movement and not appear too rigid. It is essential that construction is neat and secure, as the bouquet will have a lot of handling.

Step-by-step

Level of difficulty

Mechanics and sundries ★★

Arranging ★★★

Flowers and foliage

- 10 stems of linear foliage such as *Danae racemosa* (soft ruscus) or *Eucalyptus*
- 5–9 stems of a second foliage such as *Rosmarinus* (rosemary) to give contrast of texture
- 7 medium round flowers such as *Cymbidium* orchid heads, *Dianthus* (carnation), mini *Gerbera* or *Rosa*. Roses are the flowers referred to in the following method.
- 3–5 stems of supporting flowers such as *Eustoma* (lisianthus), *Freesia*, small orchids, spray *Dianthus* (carnation) or spray *Rosa*
- 3–8 stems of spray filler flowers such as *Alchemilla mollis* (lady's mantle), *Aster* (September flower), *Chamelaucium* (waxflower), *Gypsophila* (baby's breath), *Hypericum* (St. John's wort) or *Solidago* (golden rod)

Mechanics and sundries

- foam wedding bouquet holder – my preference is for the OASIS® 'Wedding Belle' but there are many others with a cage over the foam
- bouquet stand or tall vase filled with sand to keep it stable – the bouquet handle can be placed over the vase opening and taped in place to stop it moving around
- 1m (3ft 3in) length of 2.5cm (1in) satin ribbon (optional)
- florist's cold glue or glue dots
- thin plastic film
- long 0.56 and 0.71 wires
- tissue paper for storage (optional)

Note

The wiring methods used in a semi-wired bouquet are as described on pages 190–191 as the stems are extended not removed.

Note

The drawing below shows the outline and main placements as detailed in the following pages.

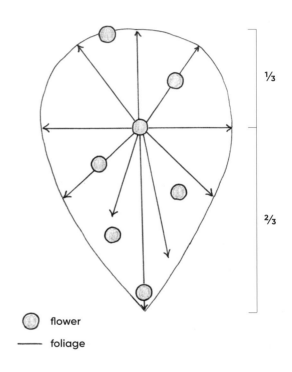

⅓

⅔

○ flower

—— foliage

METHOD

1 Dip the foam holder in water and hold for several seconds, then shake off any excess. Alternatively, spray the foam with water. Do not over-soak.

2 Place the holder on a bouquet stand or in a tall, heavy vase or container. Ideally, the foam head of the holder should be about chin high.

3 You can ribbon the handle at this stage or leave it to the end. Place a dab of florist's glue or glue dot at the top of the handle. Adhere ribbon to the glue and wind down the handle to the end. Finish with more glue to hold the ribbon in place. Cover with cling film until the point of delivery.

4 Create an outline of foliage in a teardrop shape. The foliage and flowers that are angled downwards out of the holder need to be wired for security. Exceptions can be made with very light stems if you wish. You can also wire the stems placed horizontally to give extra security.

5 Start at the bottom and insert the first stem (a) vertically upwards. This should be wired with a single-leg mount on an existing stem (see page 190). This stem will establish the finished length of the bouquet. Take the length of wire attached to the bottom part of the stem through the foam at the lowest possible point of the wedding bouquet holder and out the other side. The stem of the foliage should go about 2.5cm (1in) into the foam. Cut the wire that has come through the holder to about 2.5cm (1in) and bend it over the plastic caging and back into the foam. This stem should naturally arch outwards and curve back in towards the knee.

6 Position additional wired stems (b) and (c), using the same single-leg mount technique, one each side of the first stem that was placed vertically downwards. Using the same technique as in the previous step, take the wire through the foam and out the other side, then tuck the cut wire end back into the foam. These two stems, which will vary in length, should fit within the teardrop shape.

7 Now add the horizontal side pieces (d), one out of each side. These should be placed above the central band of plastic and angled slightly backwards. They can be wired or unwired – your choice, but I prefer the extra security given by wiring. The two arms should be of equal length. The overall width of the bouquet should be about 35cm (14in), depending on the wishes of the bride. Allowing for the width of the foam in the holder and the amount of stem that goes in the foam, a rough estimate for the visible length of each horizontal stem is about 12.5cm (5in).

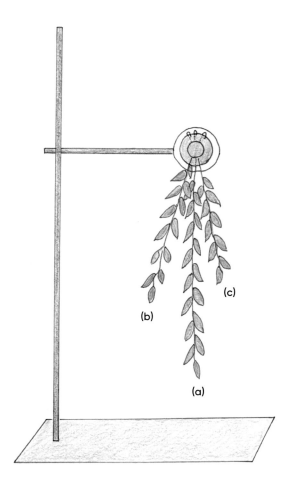

8 Place a stem vertically (e) out of the top part of the foam holder close to the base ring of plastic. This should be angled slightly backwards. This stem does not need to be wired. In order to give good proportions, its length will be about one-third that of the first downward stem that you placed.

9 Fill in the outline to create an evenly spaced teardrop shape.

11 Select the largest rose and set aside.

12 Reinforce the length of the bouquet with one of the roses (A). It should be nearly as long as the longest stem of foliage that was placed first. This flower must be wired. Measure it against the foliage before cutting. It needs to be just shorter than the longest stem of foliage placed vertically downwards. Wire the rose with a single-leg mount and insert the wire through the holder and out at the top. Make sure the end of the stem end, not just the wire, is in the foam about 2.5cm (1in). Cut the wire short and turn the end back into the foam over the lowest section of plastic caging.

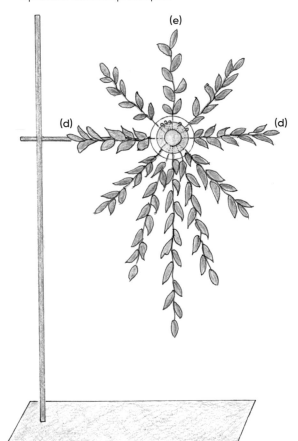

reinforce the shape with a second foliage

10 Reinforce the shape with the second foliage, in this case *Rosmarinus*, with the single-leg-mount technique, using 0.56 mm wires for the pieces angled downwards. Those positioned elsewhere do not need to be wired. Place the stems low in the holder and angle them slightly backwards. Leave the centre empty.

13 The second rose (B) should be wired and positioned so that it is angled downwards to one side to the first rose. It will be shorter than the first rose. Position it in the same direction as the shorter foliage stem.

14 Place the third rose (C) on the opposite side at a slightly higher angle. This should also be wired.

15 Now take the largest rose that you had set aside. Place this fourth flower (D) in the centre of the foam – right in the bullseye. The angle should be in line with the handle.

16 Position the fifth rose (E) in the bottom half of the bouquet, on the same side as (B) but slightly higher filling the space in the lower half.

17 The sixth rose (F) should be placed high, in a diagonal line with (E) and (D).

18 The seventh rose (G) is placed at the back on the perimeter of the return section of the bouquet. Think of five minutes to the hour on a clock face. This is an important flower as it is the one the bride sees as she holds her bouquet.

19 If you wish to have nine rather than seven focal flowers use the two extra flowers to fill in any gaps. These gaps are usually below the bullseye on the left and at the top right. All focal flowers should be more or less the same distance apart.

EXPERT TIPS

- If you make a larger hole than necessary when placing your central flower and it wobbles insert a small length of stem alongside the flower so the hole is filled.

- From time to time take the bouquet off the stand and hold it in front of a mirror to assess the line and balance. A well-balanced bouquet feels light and easy to hold.

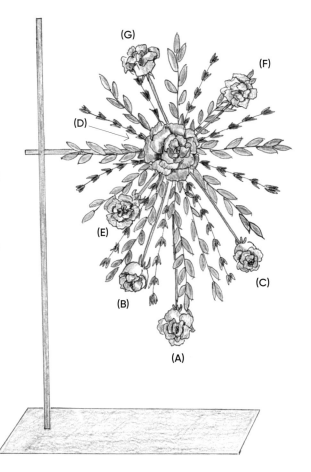

20 Fill in with your supporting flowers. Place a stem at the top (12 o'clock) and then follow round to reinforce the outline of the foliage. Never exceed your foliage outline. Then add through the established lines of the bouquet, balancing the placements at all times. Remember, all stems angled downwards need to be wired unless they are very light. Be sure to angle stems backwards to keep a lovely domed appearance so that it looks good from the sides as well as the front.

21 You may now wish to add more foliage around the central area. The foliage should be quite short so that it does not overpower the flowers.

22 Add your spray filler flowers. If they are light you may not need to wire them even if they are placed downwards.

23 Check your bouquet to make sure that you do not have any gaps and fill in if necessary.

24 Lightly mist the bouquet. Give protection by covering with a piece of tissue paper. Store in a cool place.

EXPERT TIPS

- If you use *Danae racemosa* (soft ruscus) and you have small subsidiary branches twirl these around the main stem you are using to make a stronger line. As an alternative, you can catch the leaves onto another piece of foliage to fill in any gaps.

- You can glue small leaves over the white plastic of the bouquet holder at the top of the handle to conceal it.

- If any rose protrudes too much use a very fine silver wire and attach the stem to a piece of foliage. Ensure that you cut the wire so that the ends do not catch on the bride's dress.

RIGHT A semi-wired bouquet using large individual *Eustoma* (lisianthus) heads for the focal flowers, complemented by *Alchemilla mollis* (lady's mantle), *Freesia*, *Hypericum* (St. John's wort) and *Veronica*, with *Asparagus setaceus* and *Eucalyptus parviflora*.

Designer: Neil Bain

DESIGNS FOR BRIDESMAIDS

Bridesmaids' bouquets are often a smaller version of the bride's but there are other designs that are simple to make and easy to carry that would be eminently suitable.

Hand-tied bouquet

A bridesmaid's hand-tied bouquet is usually a smaller version of the bride's.

RIGHT An autumnal bridesmaid's posy with a beautiful rich colour palette of seasonal flowers including *Allium*, *Astrantia*, *Hypericum* (St. John's wort), *Rosa* 'Cherry Brandy' and *Zantedeschia* 'Mango' (calla).
Designer: Jane Maples

LEFT Rachel's wedding bouquet is shown on page 249. Her bridesmaids had similar bouquets that were about 25 per cent smaller than her own.
Designer: Judith Blacklock

FOLLOWING PAGE ▶ A bevy of beautiful bridesmaids carrying a smaller version of the bride's bouquet of *Alchemilla mollis* (lady's mantle) and *Rosa* 'O'Hara', with *Mentha* (mint) and *Rosmarinus*.
Designer: Judith Blacklock

Pomander

A pomander is a charming floral decoration for bridesmaids, who will find it fun and easy to carry. Larger versions are also suitable for the bride, who will likewise find it easy to carry. The sphere may be covered with leaves, flower heads or a mix of flowers and foliage. Using only one type of a small round flower, such as spray *Rosa* or single white blooms of spray *Chrysanthemum*, looks particularly effective. Small, flat flowers and dense, small-leaved foliage such as *Asparagus umbellatus* (ming fern), *Buxus* (box) or *Hebe* help to retain a spherical shape. Sweet-smelling herbs such as *Myrtus communis* (common myrtle) or short sprigs of *Rosmarinus* (rosemary) give fragrance. In season, when they are mature and strong, florets of *Hydrangea* look great.

When making a pomander, it is easier if you have access to a bouquet stand, from which the sphere can be hung while inserting the materials. A small-necked vase, upon which the design can sit while you work, would suffice. The finished design needs to be as light as possible so the minimum amount of strain is put on the loop. A quick dip in water prior to starting, plus a spray on completion, should be sufficient to keep the plant material fresh for at least a day.

LEFT A pomander of spray single *Chrysanthemum* and *Asparagus umbellatus* (ming fern).
Designer: Judith Blacklock

Step-by-step

Level of difficulty
Mechanics and sundries ★★
Arranging ★★

Flowers and foliage
- 8–10 stems of spray *Rosa*
- 3–4 stems of *Asparagus umbellatus* (ming fern) or 10 stems of *Rosmarinus* (rosemary) cut into short lengths

Mechanics and sundries
- 9cm (4in) foam sphere
- 30cm (12in) length of 2.5cm (1in) satin ribbon or 45cm (18in) length if you would like tails
- 0.46 or 0.56 wire
- stem tape
- long 0.71 wire: 46 cm (18in)
- small square or circle of cellophane
- pot tape (optional)
- cold glue (optional)

METHOD

1 Spray the foam with water or dip it in water for just a couple of seconds. If the sphere is soaked thoroughly it will be too heavy and the handle will not be sufficiently secure.

2 Fold 30cm (12in) of ribbon in half to make the handle. Tightly wrap a 0.46 or 0.56 wire round both cut ends using a double-leg mount. Tape. Alternatively knot the ribbon ends and take a wire through or over the knot.

3 Bend the 0.71 wire in two and place it against the top of the existing taped wire. Tape down about 5cm (2in), leaving the two wire ends exposed. These should be cut to an equal length but left long.

4 Place a small square or circle of cellophane on the sphere to stop the damp foam touching the ribbon.

5 Push the wires through the sphere until the two ends emerge from the other side, hopefully in close proximity. If the wires decide to wander have another go, as it does not always work first time.

6 To keep the ribbon handle secure under pressure wedge a short, strong piece of stem, such as that from a rose, between the two wire ends that have emerged at the base of the sphere. Push it slightly into the foam. Bend the two lengths of wire over the short length of stem and back into the foam. You may need to trim the wires a little to make insertion into the foam easier. As an alternative you can use a cross of pot tape or a dab of cold glue over the point where the wires exit the foam to give additional security.

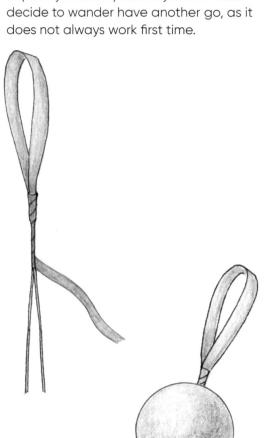

7 If you wish to add a tail to the base of the pomander take a second length of ribbon, fold it in two and wire and tape the folded area to make two tails. Insert the wires in the base of the sphere opposite the handle. The tail is not weight-bearing, so the wire stems need only be inserted firmly in the foam without additional gluing.

8 Cut the heads of the flowers and foliage short and insert in the foam. I start with the flowers and evenly distribute them over the foam. I then fill in with short sprigs of foliage.

9 Spray with water and keep in a cool place.

EXPERT TIPS

- For a low-budget pomander you could cover the sphere with squares of long-lasting leaves such as *Eucalyptus*, *Hedera helix* (ivy) or *Ruscus hypoglossum* (hard ruscus) secured with pretty pins, perhaps with a flourish of flowers at the top.

- If the sphere is too large rub it between your hands and it will reduce quickly and easily to the size you require. Take care to wash your hands after doing this before touching your eyes.

- If you are using round flowers such as *Rosa* the overall size of the pomander will end up much larger than the size of the sphere used.

- A 7cm (3in) or 9cm (4in) sphere is perhaps the most useful size, but as a general guide go smaller rather than larger. Keep the size in harmony with the person for whom it is intended.

- If you wish to cover a 9cm (4in) pomander with spray *Rosa* you will need about 15–20 stems and with *Gypsophila* about 20–25 stems. Covering with spray *Chrysanthemum* is a cheaper option and also looks lovely.

RIGHT A pomander of spray *Rosa* 'Jana' and *Asparagus umbellatus* (ming fern).

Designer: Judith Blacklock

Hoop

A hoop is easy to carry and looks lovely in the hands of young bridesmaids. Metal hoops can be purchased and then decorated. Those with a natural base are inexpensive to make and always look charming. The size needs to be appropriate for the height and age of the bridesmaids.

Step-by-step

Level of difficulty

Mechanics and sundries ★

Arranging ★

Flowers and foliage

- flexible stems such as *Cornus* (dogwood),) *Kerria japonica* or *Salix* (willow) that can be easily stripped of leaves, tightly bound flowering *Genista* (broom) or *Schoenus melanostacys* (flexi-grass)
- 3–4 trails of *Hedera helix* (ivy), *Jasminum* (jasmine), *Danae racemosa* (soft ruscus) or any other trailing plant material

Mechanics and sundries

- bindwire
- wire and stem tape
- 50–70cm (20–28in) length of 2.5cm (1in) satin ribbon

METHOD

1 Make a circle of the required size with one or two flexible stems. Secure in place with bindwire.

2 Bring in other stems and secure to make a hoop of the desired width. Try to choose stems of equal thickness.

3 Take a length of *Danae racemosa* or any trailing plant material, wrap it round the hoop and secure with bindwire. Leave a section at the top uncovered if you wish to add ribbon at the holding point.

4 Wire and tape a few flowers such as spray *Dianthus* (carnation), *Eustoma* (lisianthus), *Hypericum* (St. John's wort) or orchids and attach discreetly.

5 Wrap ribbon around the top of the hoop so it is about 12.5cm (5in) in width and finish with a neat bow. Overlap 50 per cent of each wrap as you go.

EXPERT TIP

- You could add a loop of ribbon as a handle so the hoop is less likely to get lost during the day. Wire to the top of the hoop before decorating.

RIGHT The basic framework for this hoop was constructed from two 0.90 wires taped together. It was then wrapped tightly with ribbon to conceal the mechanics and a ribbon handle was added. Two wired corsages of *Allium*, *Eustoma* (lisianthus), spray *Rosa* and *Viburnum opulus* 'Roseum', with *Danae racemosa* (soft ruscus) and *Xerophyllum tenax* (bear grass), were created separately and then taped and bound onto the framework so the hoop could be viewed from both sides.

Designer: Sarah Hills-Ingyon

ABOVE A hoop with a difference. Sarah looped and layered dried flat midelino canes and *Typha* leaves to create the circular hoop shape which was bound with raffia at the top. *Tillandsia xerographica* leaf was allowed to curl round the design and *Ceropegia linearis* subsp. *woodii* (sweetheart vine) and *Senecio rowleyanus* (string of pearls) were glued between the layers of the hoop. *Helleborus* blooms created a feature at the top.

Designer: Sarah Hills-Ingyon

Basket design

A basket of flowers is a delightful yet easy arrangement for a bridesmaid to hold, but it must be the right size. It looks lovely filled with fresh flowers and foliage, but dried or silk flowers could also be used.

This step-by-step design has been made for a bridesmaid to carry at a summer wedding in a basket that has an open weave. The method of securing the mechanics is neat and unobtrusive.

BELOW The low handle meant that the flowers needed to be kept low and compact. *Astrantia*, spray *Dianthus* (carnation) and *Gypsophila* (baby's breath) were packed closely together on a base of *Pittosporum tenuifolium*. The handle was ribboned and two bows were added to give a delicate air.

Designer: Dawn Jennings

Step-by-step

Level of difficulty

Mechanics and sundries ★★

Arranging ★★

Flowers and foliage

- flowing foliage such as *Danae racemosa* (soft ruscus), *Eucalyptus* or *Hedera helix* (ivy)
- foliage with contrasting texture
- round flowers such as *Centaurea* (cornflower), *Gerbera*, mini *Helianthus* (sunflower), *Paeonia*, *Rosa* or open *Tulipa*
- filler flowers such as *Bouvardia*, *Dianthus* (spray carnation), *Dianthus barbatus* (sweet William), *Eustoma* (lisianthus), *Freesia*, *Gypsophila* (baby's breath) or *Veronica*

Mechanics and sundries

- floral foam
- thin plastic film
- small container
- pot tape
- basket about 20cm (8in) in length with a tall handle
- 2 x 45cm (18in) lengths of 0.90 wire

EXPERT TIPS

- Ribbon can be twisted around the handle or satin bows tied to its base to link with the colour of the bridesmaids' dresses. The basket could also be prepared this way if being used to hold rose petals for throwing.
- The plastic container could be a recycled food container or an aerosol-can lid.
- For larger baskets bring the attachment wires over the pot tape so that the wire does not cut through the foam.

METHOD

1 Cover the bottom of the foam with thin plastic film to come halfway up the sides.

2 Soak the foam and place in the small container. Take pot tape over the foam so that it is well secured.

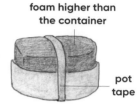

foam higher than the container

pot tape

3 Place the container in the centre of the basket. The foam should rise higher than the rim.

4 Tape both 0.90 wires, then bend each into a 'U' shape. Take the two ends of the first wire through the basket weave at the side of the small container. Repeat at the other side with the second wire. Bring the four wire ends up and over the top of the foam and then down deep into the foam. If the wires are not sufficiently long attach extra wires with tape.

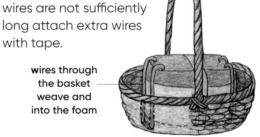

wires through the basket weave and into the foam

5 Insert the foliage outline following the shape of the basket. Reinforce the shape with a foliage with a contrasting texture.

6 Add the focal flowers through the design and fill in with less dominant flowers.

BELOW A woven basket was filled with *Alchemilla mollis* (lady's mantle), spray *Chrysanthemum* 'Stallion', *Dianthus barbatus* 'Green Trick' (carnation), spray *Dianthus* (spray carnation), *Eustoma* (lisianthus) and *Tulipa*, on a base of *Danae racemosa* (soft ruscus) and *Eucalyptus cinerea*.

Designer: Judith Blacklock

EXPERT TIPS

- If the basket does not have an open weave you could simply glue the dish to the base of the basket.

- Remember to leave enough room between the flowers and the handle so that the basket can be carried easily.

This practical reference guides you to the most effective wiring technique(s) for many of the flowers mentioned together with illustrated descriptions of the tools of the trade – many of which are cross-referenced in this book.

PRACTICAL
REFERENCE GUIDE

WIRING GUIDE

This is a guide to the methods you could use to wire the flowers listed below, but do consider the size and weight of each flower and the fact that various methods will often achieve the same objective.

Wiring techniques when the natural stem is reduced considerably in length

Internal wiring with single or double crossing of wire through the seed box

PURPOSE To reduce the weight and make manipulation easy when using light or medium single-headed flowers with solid stems that have a defined seed box below the petals. It can also be used for the larger heads of a spray flower.

SUITABLE FOR
- *Centaurea* (cornflower)
- *Dahlia* (dahlia)
- *Dianthus* (spray carnation)
- *Dianthus* (standard bloom carnation)
- *Gerbera* and mini *Gerbera*
- *Rosa* (rose)

Single-leg mount

PURPOSE To support delicate, branching forms singly or in a bunch to make one unit.

SUITABLE FOR
- *Acacia* (mimosa)
- *Achillea* (yarrow)
- *Alchemilla* (lady's mantle)
- *Asclepias* (butterfly weed)
- *Astilbe* (false goat's beard)
- *Astrantia* (Hattie's pincushion)
- *Bouvardia* (bouvardia)
- *Bupleurum* (hare's ear root)
- *Carthamus* (safflower)
- *Chamelaucium* (waxflower)
- *Eryngium* (sea holly)
- *Gypsophila* (baby's breath)
- *Hylotelephium* (sedum, ice plant)
- *Hypericum* (rose of Sharon, St. John's wort)
- *Jasminum* (jasmine)
- *Limonium* (sea lavender, winged statice)
- *Mentha* (mint)
- *Origanum* (wild marjoram)
- *Oxypetalum* (milkweed)
- *Phlox* (phlox)
- *Retama* (bridal veil, broom)
- *Skimmia* (skimmia)
- *Solidago* (golden rod)
- *Trachelium* (throatwort)

Double-leg mount

PURPOSE To support and control heavy, solid flowers with impenetrable woody stems and no calyx.

SUITABLE FOR

- *Agapanthus* (African lily)
- *Allium* (ornamental onion)
- *Alpinia* (ginger)
- *Amaranthus* (love-lies-bleeding)
- *Anthurium* (painter's palette)
- *Anthirrhinum* (snapdragon)
- *Banksia* (firewood banksia, odd brush)
- *Brassica* (ornamental cabbage)
- *Celosia* (crested and plumed cockscomb)
- *Chrysanthemum* (single-headed bloom, 'mum')
- *Curcuma* (Siam tulip, summer tulip, Thai tulip)
- *Cynara* (cardoon)
- *Dahlia* (dahlia)
- *Delphinium* (delphinium)
- *Digitalis* (foxglove)
- *Eremurus* (foxtail lily)
- *Forsythia* (forsythia)
- *Fritillaria* (fritillary)
- *Gladiolus* (gladiolus)
- *Hedera helix* 'Arborescens' (fruiting tree ivy)
- *Helianthus* (sunflower)
- *Heliconia* (lobster claw)
- *Leucadendron* (conebush)
- *Leucospermum* (nutan, pincushion protea)
- *Liatris* (gayfeather)
- *Lilium* (all varieties)
- *Matthiola* (stock)
- *Paeonia* (peony)
- *Polianthes* (tuberose)
- *Protea* (protea)
- *Salix* (pussy willow)
- *Strelitzia* (bird-of-paradise)
- *Syringa* (lilac)
- *Viburnum opulus* 'Roseum' (guelder rose, snowball tree)

Clustering

PURPOSE To make a single unit from a bunch of delicate, branching forms.

SUITABLE FOR

- *Acacia* (mimosa)
- *Achillea* (yarrow)
- *Alchemilla* (lady's mantle)
- *Alstroemeria* (Peruvian lily)
- *Asclepias* (butterfly weed)
- *Astilbe* (false goat's beard)
- *Astrantia* (Hattie's pincushion)
- *Bouvardia* (bouvardia)
- *Bupleurum* (hare's ear root)
- *Chamelaucium* (waxflower)
- *Gypsophila* (baby's breath)
- *Hedera helix* 'Arborescens' (tree ivy)
- *Jasminum* (jasmine)
- *Limonium* (sea lavender, winged statice)
- *Myosotis* (forget-me-not)
- *Origanum* (wild marjoram)
- *Oxypetalum* (milkweed)
- *Solidago* (golden rod)
- *Stephanotis* (bridal wreath, Madagascar jasmine)
- *Tanacetum* (feverfew)
- *Trachelium* (throatwort)

Hook wiring

PURPOSE A quick and easy way to wire flowers with a mass of petals and no pronounced centre. It is also used for stems that are soft and/or hollow.

SUITABLE FOR

- *Anemone* (anemone)
- *Calendula* (pot marigold)
- *Chrysanthemum* spray ('mum')
- *Dahlia* (dahlia)
- *Dianthus* (spray carnation)
- *Dianthus* (standard bloom carnation)
- *Gerbera* and mini *Gerbera* (South African daisy)
- *Ranunculus* (turban flower)

Wiring individual florets or pips

PURPOSE To incorporate individual florets from a stem bearing multiple flowers into small, delicate wired designs. The florets need to be volumetric, which means they have space within the flower.

SUITABLE FOR

- *Agapanthus* (African lily)
- *Alstroemeria* (Peruvian lily)
- *Anthirrhinum* (snapdragon)
- *Aquilegia* (colombine, granny's bonnet)
- *Campanula* (Canterbury bell)
- *Clematis* (clematis)
- *Convallaria* (lily-of-the-valley)
- *Crocosmia* (montbretia)
- *Delphinium* (delphinium)
- *Digitalis* (foxglove)
- *Eucharis amazonica* (Amazon lily, Eucharist lily)
- *Eustoma* (lisianthus)
- *Forsythia* (forsythia)
- *Freesia* (freesia)
- *Fritillaria* (fritillary)
- *Gentiana* (gentian)
- *Gladiolus* (gladiolus)
- *Hyacinthoides* (Spanish bluebell)
- *Hyacinthus* (hyacinth)
- *Jasminum* (jasmine)
- *Nerine* (Guernsey lily)
- *Ornithogalum* (chincherinchee)
- *Polianthes* (tuberose)
- *Prunus* (cherry blossom, peach blossom)
- *Sandersonia* (Christmas bells)
- *Stephanotis* (bridal wreath, Madagascar jasmine)
- *Triteleia* (brodia)

Support wiring techniques for longer stems and to make them flexible

Single-leg mount

PURPOSE To extend the length of stem of light plant material and/or secure/control in a design.

SUITABLE FOR

- *Acacia* (mimosa)
- *Achillea* (yarrow)
- *Alchemilla* (lady's mantle)
- *Asclepias* (butterfly weed)
- *Astilbe* (false goat's beard)
- *Astrantia* (Hattie's pincushion)
- *Bouvardia* (bouvardia)
- *Bupleurum* (hare's ear root)
- *Chamelaucium* (waxflower)
- *Eryngium* (sea holly)
- *Euphorbia esula* (green spurge, leafy spurge)
- *Gypsophila* (baby's breath)
- *Hylotelephium* (sedum, ice plant)
- *Hypericum* (rose of Sharon, St. John's wort)
- *Jasminum* (jasmine)
- *Limonium* (sea lavender, winged statice)
- *Mentha* (mint)
- *Origanum* (wild marjoram)
- *Oxypetalum* (milkweed)
- *Phlox* (phlox)
- *Retama* (bridal veil, broom)
- *Skimmia* (skimmia)
- *Solidago* (golden rod)
- *Trachelium* (throatwort)

Double-leg mount

PURPOSE To extend the length of heavier plant material with impenetrable woody stems and no calyx to secure and/or control in a design.

SUITABLE FOR
- *Agapanthus* (African lily)
- *Allium* (ornamental onion)
- *Alpinia* (ginger)
- *Amaranthus* (love-lies-bleeding)
- *Ammi* (lace flower, Queen Anne's lace)
- *Anthurium* (painter's palette)
- *Anthirrhinum* (snapdragon)
- *Banksia* (firewood banksia, odd brush)
- *Brassica* (ornamental cabbage)
- *Celosia* (crested and plumed cockscomb)
- *Chrysanthemum* (single-headed bloom, 'mum')
- *Curcuma* (Siam tulip, summer tulip, Thai tulip)
- *Cynara* (cardoon)
- *Dahlia* (dahlia)
- *Delphinium* (delphinium)
- *Digitalis* (foxglove)
- *Eremurus* (foxtail lily)
- *Forsythia* (forsythia)
- *Fritillaria* (fritillary)
- *Gladiolus* (gladiolus)
- *Hedera helix* 'Arborescens' (fruiting tree ivy)
- *Helianthus* (sunflower)
- *Heliconia* (lobster claw)
- *Leucadendron* (conebush)
- *Leucospermum* (nutan, pincushion protea)
- *Liatris* (gayfeather)
- *Lilium* (lily)
- *Matthiola* (stock)
- *Paeonia* (peony)
- *Polianthes* (tuberose)
- *Protea* (protea)
- *Salix* (pussy willow)
- *Strelitzia* (bird-of-paradise)
- *Syringa* (lilac)
- *Viburnum opulus* 'Roseum' (guelder rose, snowball tree)

Winding

PURPOSE To strengthen, support and control stems of delicate linear flowers.

SUITABLE FOR
- *Aquilegia* (colombine, granny's bonnet)
- *Convallaria* (lily-of-the-valley)
- *Freesia* (freesia)
- *Jasminum* (jasmine)
- *Lathyrus* (sweet pea)
- *Myosotis* (forget-me-not)
- *Nigella* (love-in-a-mist)
- *Stephanotis* (bridal wreath, Madagascar jasmine)

Spiralling or semi-internal

PURPOSE To prevent flower heads snapping off from soft stems and to make them easier to manipulate.

SUITABLE FOR
- *Eucharis amazonica* (Amazon lily, Eucharist lily)
- *Gerbera* and mini *Gerbera* (South African daisy)
- *Muscari* (grape hyacinth)
- *Tulipa* (tulip)
- *Zantedeschia* (calla)

TOOLS OF THE TRADE

All the tools and equipment mentioned in the book are described here in more detail. All should be available online.

Equipment and products to prepare stems for a longer life

Buckets

Round black buckets are easy to find and inexpensive to purchase. The standard round bucket is 40cm (16in) high. If you can, but they are difficult to source, try to obtain 'Dutch' buckets from your florist or wholesaler. They are cream-coloured, 38cm (15in) high and 35cm (14in) wide, with a stable, rectangular base. You can also purchase an extension that fits in the top of the bucket to give taller sides.

Cut flower food

Adding cut flower food to water allows flowers to develop fully and last longer. There are also special foods available for bulb flowers, woody stems and others. They really do work and extend life by up to 30 per cent.

Florist's knife

In the hands of an expert, a small lightweight floristry knife is a good tool for cutting stems, but for the less experienced scissors are recommended. The knife is capable of cutting both soft and semi-woody stems on a slant to expose the maximum number of cells for the easy uptake of water.

Scissors

Choose sharp scissors which will grip the stems and cut cleanly. Loop a colourful distinctive tag around the handle, as scissors are so easy to misplace. Keep a separate pair of long-bladed scissors for cutting ribbon. Avoid cutting wires with your flower scissors as this will blunt the blades. Japanese scissors are often considered the best but are usually more expensive. Keep the scissors closed when not in use.

Stem cleaner

This inexpensive, round yellow disc removes leaves and thorns from stems. It is gentle on the stems and very effective. Do not use metal strippers as they will damage stems, allowing bacteria to enter more easily.

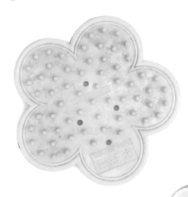

Secateurs

Quality secateurs are a must for cutting harder, woodier stems such as shrubby foliage and roses and multiple bound stems such as those in a hand-tied. There are many to choose from; select a pair that is the right size for your hand. Cut the stems on a slant.

Water misting sprays

A well-washed bottle of kitchen cleaner can be adapted for this purpose. Use it after completing or when refreshing an arrangement.

Wire cutters

You will blunt scissors very quickly if you use them to cut wire, so purchase good quality wire cutters for the job instead. Long-nosed pliers may be useful for bending wires.

Sprays for extending the life of cut flowers

There are spray products that extend the life of cut flowers and foliage and they really do work! Glory, a brand by Chrysal, is available online.

Stem supports (often referred to as mechanics)

Chicken wire/mesh wire

Chicken wire is available in three gauges, 1.25cm (½in), 2.5cm (1in) and 5cm (2in). The larger gauges are the most useful in floral design. It can be used to encase floral foam and/or moss in order to create swags and garlands. It can be scrunched up and used in vases to support flowers.

Corsage bracelet

These are very easy to use and come in a wide range of materials from Corsage Creations, available online.
They have a flat disc of Perspex to which plant material can be adhered.

Floral foam

Unlike other mechanics such as pin holders and chicken wire, floral foam also holds water. Understanding how to use it correctly is vital as otherwise your flowers will die prematurely.

Foam can be purchased in different sizes and shapes, including cylinders, balls and cones, but it comes most often in bricks. Green foam is used for arranging fresh plant material and there is a grey variety available for use with artificial and dried flowers.

Many manufacturers produce foam in different densities: a light foam for soft stems, a medium-density for general use and a premium high-density foam for heavy stems, large-scale work and for wedding bouquets, where a lot of stems go into a small piece of foam. Foam is also manufactured in larger pieces that are ideal for large-scale designs. Be careful trying to soak foam that is huge, as it will become very heavy when wet and be almost impossible to lift.

In the UK the brand leader for floral foam is OASIS®, manufactured by Smithers-Oasis. Foam is also produced by Val Spicer and Trident. In the USA brand leaders are Smithers-Oasis and Syndicate Sales which manufactures Aquafoam. In Asia one of the brand leaders is ASPAC.

Smithers-Oasis is the first manufacturer to have produced a biodegradable foam. OASIS® Bio Floral Foam Maxlife is brown in colour but is used for fresh flowers in exactly the same way as for green floral foam. It has been proven to degrade 51.5% in 365 days in biologically active landfill conditions (this just means it needs to be disposed of in your general waste). Tests are ongoing with the aim of reaching 100% biodegradability.

Designer board

These are large rectangular sheets of floral foam with a polystyrene backing. They are extremely useful when making flower walls and other big designs.

Foam bricks

Foam bricks measure 23 x 11 x 8cm (9 x 4 x 3in) and come in boxes of 20. Individual bricks may be purchased, but it is obviously more economical to buy a box.

Jumbo or large pieces of foam

Most companies manufacture foam in larger pieces than the bricks. It is sometimes referred to as Jumbo foam. These pieces are ideal for large scale work such as pedestals and urns. However a very large piece, the size of a box of 20 bricks, will get very heavy and be hard to lift and handle.

Foam hanging cages

These are trays filled with foam and covered with an open plastic cage which can be opened to replace the foam. There is a hole in the handle to make it easy to hang. Available in different sizes, they are more expensive than the basic spray trays (see page 309) but are very easy to use and can be used to create larger designs. The Smithers-Oasis version is called a Florette®.

Foam suction pads

Perfect for decorating a wedding car, these are available in various sizes and shapes in different countries. The foam is covered with plastic caging with a suction device on the base. At the time of writing they are available dome-shaped or square. They can also be fixed to any clean, dry surfaces such as glass, windows and mirrors.

Garlands

An OASIS® Netted Foam Garland consists of 12.5cm (5in) cylinders of foam held together with nylon netting which can be cut to any length. They can be arranged to fit a range of spaces, including doors and gazebos, or to create a floral arch.

The Trident Foam Ultra Garland (below) are filled with foam. The advantage is that the foam can be easily replaced and the cages reused indefinitely.

Iglu®

An Iglu® is a pre-formed dome of foam in a cage with a solid green plastic base. Two side tabs allow wire, bindwire or ribbon to be threaded through for attaching.

Mini Deco

These are 5cm (2in) diameter half-spheres of wet or dry foam on a plastic base with a self-adhesive pad on the bottom. Dip the wet foam in water, then remove the tape backing to reveal the adhesive. They are ideal for decorating a wedding cake but can also be adhered to many items such as mirrors, bottles, presents and tables.

OASIS® Mini, Medi and Maxi Table Deco

In the UK Smithers-Oasis produces these specialised forms in narrow plastic bases. They are sold in three lengths, all of which are ideal for long, slender displays of flowers.

Posy Pads

Posy pads are available with a diameter of between 10 and 40cm (4 and 16in) with a plastic or polystyrene base. The plastic base has a small lip to prevent dripping. Leaves or ribbon can be pinned to those with a polystyrene base. They are an excellent mechanic to place on the top of a tall vase.

Rings

Foam rings have a diameter of between 20 and 61cm (8 and 24in). They can be purchased with a plastic or polystyrene base. The plastic base has a lip to prevent dripping. Leaves can be pinned to those with a polystyrene base. Rings are useful as hanging designs, as table centrepieces filled with candles or to encircle the base of a candelabrum.

Spheres

Foam spheres are available in a wide range of sizes from 7 – 25cm (3 – 10in). They are ideal for topiary or hanging designs. You can also purchase spheres encased in green nylon netting, which gives extra support. Wire or twine can be used to suspend the sphere to create a hanging ball of flowers.

Wedding bouquet holders

Most bouquet holders have a plastic handle with a section of wet or dry foam encased on top into which stems are inserted. The holders come in various shapes and sizes. The larger the piece of foam the bigger the finished design will be. Holders containing grey dry foam are also available for silk flower bouquets.

SOAKING FOAM

To soak foam correctly for fresh plant material, so that every molecule is full of water, fill a basin or bowl that is deeper and wider than the piece you wish to soak. To prevent dry patches (which will not supply the flowers with water) you should gently place the foam on the surface of still water. It will sink under its own weight until the foam is level with the water and the colour has changed from light to dark green or brown to dark brown. A brick will take about 50 seconds to soak. High-density foams will take longer but you should follow the same procedure.

For details on how to soak bouquet holders see page 274.

STORING FOAM

If after use your foam is still intact with only a few holes you could keep it for future use. Place it in a plastic bag and tie firmly so that it is airtight, which will conserve the moisture. Once it has been wetted, the foam must not be allowed to dry out as it will not take up water effectively. If it is dry, it must be discarded.

Gel beads

These tiny beads in a vast array of colours are sold in small packets. There is also a larger bead gel available – again in a wide range of colours – which will create marble-sized gel balls once water is added. They are hard to dispose of and should not be washed down the sink, outside drain or toilet.

Glass nuggets and stone aggregates (pebbles and gravel)

Glass nuggets and aggregates may be used in glass containers and vases to support stems, while also being decorative. They can be purchased in net bags and jars in a range of colours and natural/colourless forms.

Pin holders

A pin holder can be used again and again. It consists of numerous pins embedded in a lead base that is designed to support stems. It is ideal for woody, soft and hollow stems.

Pin holders come in a range of sizes and shapes although 6cm (2½in) is the most commonly available and perhaps the most useful. In the USA a pin holder is sometimes referred to as a frog and in Asia as a kenzan.

Containers and stands

Candelabrum

Candelabra are usually black or silver. The black ones do get marked quite easily so I prefer to use silver. It is possible to hire candelabra at a daily rate, but this can work out more expensive than anticipated as you will probably need them for more than one day, so purchasing may be the best solution if you have space for storage.

Candelabra can be purchased with arms in different positions, so the method of decoration will need to be adjusted.

Candle cup

This is a small plastic cup, with a protrusion from the base, that holds foam. It is designed for inserting into candlesticks, candelabra and bottles in order to create a raised arrangement. An alternative is to glue a cork to the bottom of a round plastic dish.

Glass vases

Glass vases look wonderful in contemporary work singly or grouped. The best-quality glass is usually the heaviest glass. For general flower work the optimum vase height is about 20cm (8in). When carrying glass always use two hands to support both the top and the bottom to avoid breakages and injuries.

Tall slim glass vases (often referred to as lily vases) can create impressive floral displays in the centre of tables, but make sure they are sufficiently tall and slender not to impede the view of anyone sitting at the table. Vases that are 80cm (31½ in) or taller are best. Also ensure they are weighted or filled with water and therefore stable in a public environment.

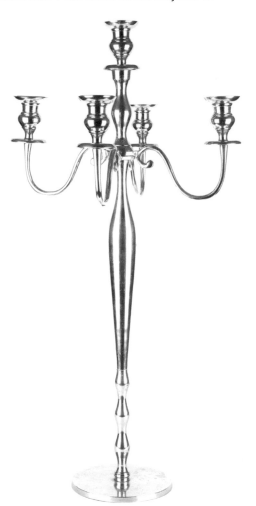

Florist's trays

Florist's plastic trays can be used for a variety of arrangements such as those for long, narrow ledges and mantelpieces. They can also be used in a row along a trestle table. They are available in three lengths (taking one, two or three bricks of foam) in black, green and white. They can be spray painted to tone with any design scheme if necessary.

Pedestal stands/plinths

If acquiring these for the first time avoid very flimsy decorative ironwork pedestals as they can look inadequate if supporting a large arrangement of flowers and foliage. Solid plinths may be more expensive but they look stronger and give better stability. These are usually used for designs that are front-facing but also enjoyed from the two sides.

An urn on a plinth is ideal for an arrangement in the round so is usually placed away from the wall. Fibreglass urns and plinths are excellent as they are light, stable and look extremely good.

Pot bulb bowls

Plastic pot bulb bowls are easy to clean, inexpensive and easily hidden by plant material. They are available in a range of sizes and are available from garden centres, DIY centres, craft stores and some florists. They can hold arrangements of all sizes, from a small table design to a large pedestal. They can be easily covered with double-sided tape and strong leaves.

Spray trays with handle for hanging

Sometimes known as pew ends or shovels, these rectangular plastic trays with a handle are invaluable. They are similar to foam hanging cages (see page 303) but are considerably less expensive. They are also available with a foam insertion covered with a plastic cage. These are available in various sizes and are useful for large-scale work.

Extension tubes/cones

Plastic extension tubes/cones are used to raise the height of plant material so are particularly useful in pedestal, urn or column displays. They can be filled with foam, chicken wire or simply water. Metal cones are also available but are not as easy to source.

Water tubes – glass, Perspex and plastic

These provide the perfect mini vase for one or more stems. Although most cannot stand on their own they are lovely filled with water and either strapped to a structure or suspended by a hanging wire. Glass tubes look great but they do break easily; Perspex breaks less readily. Coloured and transparent plastic orchid tubes with a small hole in a plastic cap to keep stems secure are available. They can be covered with moss, long-lasting leaves, fabric or thin bark held in place with decorative wire, bindwire or raffia. Tubes with extensions are also available. Various decorative shapes can also be obtained – 'seahorses' and bubble forms (colourless).

Wedding bouquet stands

A professional wedding bouquet stand is expensive but well worth buying if you wish to make wedding flowers your profession. A cheaper alternative is to take a tall thin vase, fill it with sand for ballast and then wedge the bouquet holder in the opening.

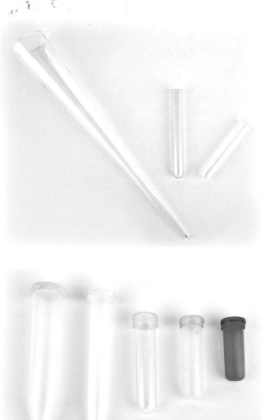

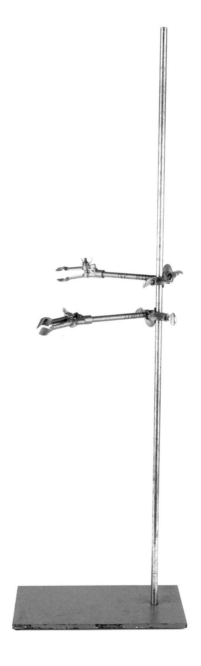

Tying, binding and securing

Bindwire

Bindwire (paper-covered wire) is ideal for hanging arrangements where wire might slip or cause damage. It is also used for binding together branches and twigs securely. It can also be made into a decorative feature. It is commonly available in two colours, green and neutral, but others can be found.

Cable ties

Cable ties in a wide range of colours and sizes are used for fastening tubes to twigs, securing large structures, keeping chicken wire firmly in position over foam and offering a decorative feature. They are invaluable as a tying mechanism for large structures such as arches. They cannot be reused.

Cocktail and kebab sticks

Cocktail and kebab sticks are used to support fruit and vegetables for inclusion in designs. Simply place the sticks in the base of your fruit or vegetable and insert the other ends in floral foam.

Double-sided tape

Double-sided tape has many uses but is ideal for attaching leaves to a plastic or glass container. It can also be used on plastic bouquet handles so that ribbon or leaves can be easily added.

Floral adhesive

Floral or cold adhesive is now used in so many designs, particularly those for adornment, and for attaching flower heads and leaves to foundations. It is a wonderful tool for the florist, expensive but well worth it. Unlike hot glue, it does not stain or burn the plant material. It is best left for a couple of minutes prior to attachment so that it becomes slightly tacky and thus adheres more effectively. If you do not have access to floral adhesive use a product such as UHU.

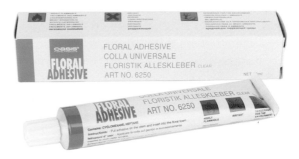

Florist's fix

This is a green, putty-like substance that is used to adhere two clean, dry surfaces together. In floristry it is often used in conjunction with a green plastic foam holder (sometimes called a frog or anchor pin) or on the base of a metal pin holder to keep foam in place.

Foam holders/frogs/anchor pin

Foam holders are light plastic discs with four prongs. They can be purchased in small and large sizes. They are ideal for keeping pieces of foam in place when used in conjunction with florist's fix, Blu-tack or similar.

Glue gun/glue pots

A glue gun is ideal for heavy-duty gluing. Sticks of glue are placed into the rear nozzle, which is then plugged into the power socket. When the trigger is pulled, heated glue is extruded from the nozzle. The glue sets almost immediately and becomes transparent. It is best used for non-fresh materials because it can leave burn marks on fresh plant material. Take care not to let hot glue drip onto skin as it will burn. Cold glue can also be used in glue guns but 'hot' is most useful for fixing heavier items.

Glue pellets are placed in the cavity in a glue pot, which is then plugged in and the glue melts. Items can be dipped into the glue.

Magnets

Metal magnets are used to attach corsages to clothing and avoids pins in delicate clothing. Always check that the recipient is not fitted with a pacemaker. They will also affect some watches.

Pins

These can be functional silver or black steel pins or decorative with a coloured head. Available in varying lengths, they are used for attaching buttonholes and corsages to lapels and ribbon onto the stems of bouquets, or for securing leaves in foam. German pins (mossing pins) are useful for securing materials into designs but you can make your own from stub wires.

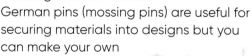

Anchor/florist's/pot tape

This is a strong tape that can be purchased in two thicknesses. It is known as anchor, florist's or pot tape. In this book it is referred to as pot tape. The wider tape keeps better and does not twist on the reel. Unlike Sellotape or Scotch tape, it adheres to wet foam. It is used primarily to keep foam securely attached to its container. There are also clear versions available for use on glass and white for wedding work and on white containers.

Raffia

Raffia is a natural fibre ideal for wrapping the stems of informal bouquets and buttonholes. It is available in many colours.

Ribbon

Available in a vast range of colours and widths, ribbon is made in a wealth of materials such as hessian, waterproof polypropylene and satin. For wedding work 2.5cm (1in) satin ribbon in cream, green and white is very useful.

Stem tape

Available in various colours, stem tape is used to conceal wires for camouflage, to cover sharp ends and to keep moisture in plant material. There are two main types on the market: Parafilm and Stemtex. More information about these tapes is given on page 196.

T-bar

A small plastic base in the shape of a 'T' with a safety pin on the back to which you can attach a corsage.

Twine/string

Twine is often used for tying stems in hand-tied bouquets. It is likely to be made of jute, a natural plant material product and can be obtained in a range of colours.

Decoration

Aluminium wire

Thick but flexible aluminium wire in metallic colours such as lime green, purple and silver gives substance and interest to contemporary designs. It can be used to make a quick and easy head piece (see page 240).

Beads and buttons

Designers often use beads to add decorative interest to arrangements. They can still be purchased from bead shops, but flower wholesalers are now selling beads in bulk. As well as providing shine and glitter, they can also be used to give detail to buttonholes and corsages threaded onto grasses.

Candles

The range of candles available is immense. There are special plastic holders available to keep candles with a 2.5 or 5cm (1 or 2in) base secure. If you do not have these holders take four-six short lengths of cocktail or kebab stick (depending on candle size), and place at an equal distance on pot tape so that only the tips are above the tape. Wrap the tape firmly around the bottom of the candle before inserting into floral foam.

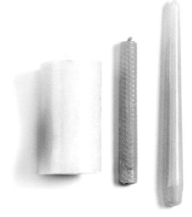

Never leave a lighted candle unattended.

Moss

Sphagnum is a natural material which retains water well and is great for covering foam for use in swag and garlands.

Leucobryum glaucum (bun moss) has a lovely soft texture and an undulating form. It is more expensive than flat moss. It is lovely used to frame flower walls.

Hypnum curvifolium (carpet or flat moss) is used to cover large areas quickly and neatly.

Preserved *Stachys* (lambs ear) leaves

These can be used to cover handles of wedding bouquets and to cover boxes and containers. They need to be secured with cold glue or double-sided tape or pinned in place.

ACKNOWLEDGEMENTS

Thank you I would like to thank my past students, friends and teachers at the school for allowing me to use images of their wedding work. They have also given me invaluable guidance and advice.

Brides and grooms A huge thank to all the brides and grooms who gave me permission to include them in the book, especially Tate Ballard and Adam Chapman, Angus and Alexandra Burrell, Jamie and Jane Flanagan, Rachel Petty, Jeff and Lucy Lu, Sam and Hannah Shutter.

Wedding cakes Former student and cake designer par excellence, Angela Veronica of the Little Pink & Wedding Shop in Evesham for her help and guidance on wedding cakes.

My students A thank you to all those listed below and in particular: Sharon Bainbridge-Clayton, Khalida Bharmal, Elizabeth Hemphill, Jane Maples, Kate Scholefield, Linda Scuizzato.

Students To all former students who have created such beauty with flowers and have been so kind as to allow me to include their work in this book: Abdulaziz Alnoman, Sharon Bainbridge-Clayton, Khalida Bharmal, Yajie Cao, June Fray, Jimmy Fu (105 Blooms), Tomoyo Fujisawa, Jo-Anne Hardy (Posy and Wild), Elizabeth Hemphill (Rose & Thistle), Catherine Macalpine (Farm to Floral), Jane Maples, Juliet Medforth, Lauren Murphy, Susan Parkinson, Karen Prendergast, Kate Scholefield (Stems of Southwater), Karen Strachan (Stems & Gems), Risa Takagi. And those from the 2018 Business Courses at the school who were willing helpers at a wedding at the Caledonian Club: Hayley Bath, Hei Laam Chang, Anusha Ekanayake, Victoria Gillespie, Yujin Hwang, Mami Kishimoto, Adrienne Monteath Van Dok, Claire Morgan, Kinuyo Okamoto.

Teachers To my wonderful team of teachers who are inspirational and inspired. They have created work for the book and have patiently checked my text for accuracy and offered invaluable advice: Neil Bain, Lynn Dallas, Mo Duffill, Sarah Hills-Ingyon, Dawn Jennings, Tomasz Koson, David Thomson, Marco Wamelink, Liz Wyatt.

Friends and colleagues from around the world have allowed me to use their wonderful designs in this book: Sue Adams, Amanda Austin Flowers, Aurelie Bolyamello, Neil Birks, Amie Bone, Jill Chant, Helen Drury, Caroline Edelin, Kath Egan, Emberton Flower Club, Leyla Fiber, June Ford-Crush, Ann-Marie French, Philip Hammond, Patricia Howe, Sabrina Heinen, Victoria Houten, Jose Hutton, Dennis Kneepkens, Julia Legg, Susan Marshall, Margaret McFarlane, Louise Roots, Tracy Rowbottom, Natalie Sakalova, Wendy Smith, Sue Smith, Glyn Spencer, Mary-Jane Vaughan, Catherine Vickers, Betty Wain, Denise Watkins, Rebecca Zhang.

Line drawings I have the greatest appreciation and respect for the coloured line drawings created by Tomoko Nakamoto, ably assisted by Ayako Yamaguchi. They gave time, effort and attention to detail to create accurate and visually beautiful work.

Venues for photography Rick Stein Restaurant Barnes, Caledonian Club, Leeds Castle, Roof Top Restaurant Kensington, St. Mary's Church Barnes, St. Paul's Church Knightsbridge, St Phillip's Church Kew.

And also: Stewart Parvin for the bridal dress on the cover

My appreciation to: Julia Harker, Tomasz Koson and Christina Turner at the flower school who have patiently smoothed the progress of this book, providing invaluable critique and assistance as it developed. I simply could not have created this book without my designer Amanda Hawkes. Her patience, professionalism and intelligence makes writing books a pleasure.

PHOTOGRAPHIC CREDITS

Sharon Bainbridge-Clayton: 206 right, 207, 211 right, 258, 271

Ian Barnes: 246

Luke Barrett: 169

Stephen Berghmans: 48

Alykhan Bharmal: 102 bottom left

Alykhan Bharmal and Hana Makovcova: 37, 58/59, 134, 182/183, 266

Judith Blacklock: 9, 23, 30, 35, 36, 42, 47, 54/55, 81, 90, 92/93, 99, 148, 151, 156, 200, 201, 202/203, 204, 205, 206 left, 209, 210 right, 211 left, 212, 213, 215, 216, 228/229, 232/233, 234/235, 236 top, 240, 268, 273, 280, 289, 293

Nikki Burke: 49

Xander Casey: 79

Thomas De Hoghton: 11, 21, 44, 45, 50, 62/63, 80, 98, 100, 105, 110/111, 116/117, 122/123, 124/125, 146 bottom, 147, 154/155, 197, 221, 225, 231, 242, 272, 279, 290

Kath Egan: 152/153

Nikki Esser: 173, 226

David Fiber: 165

Ghadeer Fadani: 129

Anna Fowler Weddings London UK: 4

June Fray: 39

Yuka Fujisaki: 245, 269

Tomoyo Fujisawa: 262

Oliver Gordon: 6, 7, 18/19, 25, 26, 28, 29, 38, 57, 74, 75, 76/77, 82/83, 84, 95, 96, 106, 107, 108/109, 112, 113, 120/121, 126/127, 137, 141, 143, 145, 157, 160/161, 210 left, 222, 223, 236 bottom, 253, 264, 282/283, 284, 287

Rebecca Gurden Photography: 248

Chrissie Harten: 60 left

David Holdsworth: 177

Neil Horne: 72/73

Patricia Howe: 43

Chris Huang: 70/71

Julia Lamont: 60/61

Leeds Castle Foundation: 32/33, 66/67, 87, 88/89, 132/133, 158/159

Sarah M Photography: 270

Pippa MacKenzie: 16

Claudia McDade: 41

Jen Meneghin: 15, 118/119, 128, 256/257

Ash Mills: 167

Murley and Maples Photography: 263, 267, 281

Mike Pannet: 27

Lisa Payne Photography: 68

Harry Richards Photography: 259, 260/261

Rebecca Robinson: 220

Jessica Roth: 102 bottom right

Sarah Jane Sanders: 139

Linda Scuizzato: 130, 131, 138, 162

September Pictures: 249

Studio 'S': 250

Steve Tanner: 65

Unique Image Photography: 243, 247

Velvet | Storm Photography: 144, 199, 227

Mark Weeks: 102/103, 146 top, 217, 219, 224, 291

Matt Wing: 254/255

Rebecca Zhang: 179

Jiaming Zhao: 189

JUDITH BLACKLOCK FLOWER SCHOOL

After reading this book you may wish to come and experience for yourself how to arrange flowers at Judith's delightful school in a flower-filled mews in the heart of Knightsbridge, London.

The school offers a wide range of courses covering almost every aspect of flowers, both as a hobby and as a profession.

Established for 16 years, it is widely acclaimed as the UK's foremost flower school. Judith is renowned worldwide for her ability to convey her knowledge to amateur and professional flower designers alike. The highly regarded courses are accredited by the British Accreditation Council (BAC) and the American Institute of Floral Designers (AIFD). There are timetables to suit all schedules and levels and online courses.

At the school, we teach in a logical, straightforward way that really does work. Once you know the techniques, we encourage you to develop your own individual style based on structured guidelines. We believe that everybody can succeed and our students prove that this is so – many now run successful flower companies or simply enjoy arranging flowers for themselves more confidently.

On longer courses we have an exceptional team of tutors who have their own particular expertise – they are both professional florists and experienced qualified tutors. Judith teaches on nearly every course, so that she can understand the aims and objectives of every student and help wherever she can.

www.judithblacklock.com

RIGHT The Judith Blacklock Flower School, London
Photograph: Lewis Khan

OTHER TITLES FROM THE FLOWER PRESS

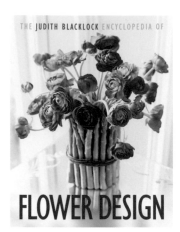

**The Judith Blacklock
Encyclopedia of Flower Design**
ISBN 978 0 9552391 0 6

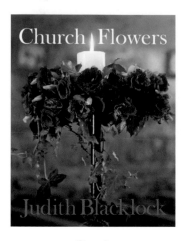

**Church
Flowers**
ISBN 978 0 9552391 6 8

**Flower Arranging
The complete guide for beginners**
ISBN 978 0 9552391 7 5

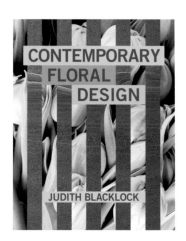

**Contemporary
Floral Design**
ISBN 978 0 9552391 9 9

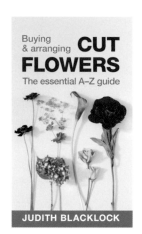

**Buying & Arranging Cut Flowers
The essential A–Z guide**
ISBN 978 0 9935715 0 3

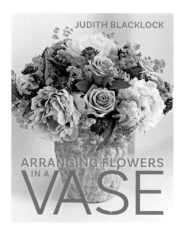

**Arranging Flowers
in a Vase**
ISBN 978 09935715 1 0

TO ORDER

Order these books through any bookshop or online retailer.
In the UK you can order direct from the publisher:
Tel: 01202 586848   www.selectps.com